NTRODUCTION

TWO OF THE MOST POPULAR TRENDS IN HOME DECORATING AND CREATIVE LIVING ARE BRINGING NATURE INTO OUR HOMES AND CREATING LIVING SPACES OUTDOORS. GARDENING AND GARDEN-RELATED MOTIFS REFLECT OUR INTEREST IN LIFESTYLES MORE CONNECTED TO NATURE AND OUR DESIRE TO NURTURE OUR SOULS THROUGH NATURE. WE YEARN TO CREATE RELAXING AND TRANQUIL SPACES WHERE WE CAN COMMUNICATE WITH NATURE.

ONE OF THE MOST REWARDING WAYS YOU CAN CELEBRATE YOUR LOVE OF THE GARDEN IS THROUGH GARDEN-INSPIRED CRAFTS. WHETHER YOU HAVE A BALCONY GARDEN WITH A FEW POTTED PLANTS, ACRES OF ROLLING FIELDS OR A SINGLE ROOM DEVOTED TO THE OUTDOORS, THIS BOOK HAS MANY FUN AND BEAUTIFUL GARDEN PROJECTS TO CREATE, SHARE AND ENJOY. IT IS MY HOPE THAT THESE PROJECTS WILL DRAW YOU CLOSER TO YOUR GARDEN AND BRING MORE OF ITS BEAUTY AND MAGIC INTO YOUR LIFE.

THE PROJECTS ARE GROUPED INTO THREE MAIN CATEGORIES BY THEME. THE FIRST THEME, *The Bountiful Garden*, USES BRIGHT COLORS AND IMAGES INSPIRED BY FRESH VEGETABLES AND FRUITS HARVESTED FROM THE GARDEN. THE PROJECTS FIT RIGHT INTO ANY CASUAL BACKYARD OR GARDEN-INSPIRED ROOM. THESE ARE GREAT PROJECTS FOR THOSE WHO LOVE TO GARDEN OR WANT TO SHARE GIFTS WITH FRIENDS WHO DO.

THE *Old World Tuscany* THEME IS REMINISCENT OF THE RENAISSANCE AND PERFECT FOR THOSE WITH FORMAL GARDENS OR WHO WANT TO ADD DRAMA TO THEIR OUTDOOR SPACES. THESE PROJECTS ARE AT HOME WHETHER DECORATING AN INDOOR ROOM OR GREETING VISITORS AT THE DOOR.

THE FUN AND FUNCTIONAL *French Botanical* THEME FITS INTO MANY GARDEN STYLES. IT'S CLASSIC YET CASUAL, INCORPORATING THE CLASS OF FRANCE AND THE CHARM OF ITS COUNTRYSIDE. THESE PROJECTS MAKE EXCELLENT GIFTS FOR ANYONE—THE GARDEN ENTHUSIAST OR THE APARTMENT DWELLER WHO ENJOYS THE ROMANCE OF A GARDEN.

ALL THE PROJECTS FEATURED IN *Inspired by the Garden* ARE FUNCTIONAL AND DESIGNED FOR INDOOR OR OUTDOOR USE. YOU'LL FIND SPECIAL CARE AND FINISHING INSTRUCTIONS TO MAKE SURE YOU CAN ENJOY YOUR PROJECTS FOR YEARS TO COME. YOU'LL ALSO SEE HANDY INFORMATION FOR PRESERVING WHAT YOUR GARDEN HAS TO OFFER, SUCH AS SAVING SEEDS, DRYING AND PRESSING FLOWERS AND KEEPING A GARDEN JOURNAL. THESE TIPS WILL HELP YOU GAIN EVEN MORE PLEASURE FROM YOUR VEGETABLE PATCH AND FLOWERBEDS. YOU WILL LEARN NEW, EASY TECHNIQUES WITH TRADITIONAL DECORATIVE TREATMENTS SUCH AS DÉCOUPAGE, MOSAICS AND STENCILING. MOST OF ALL, THE PROJECTS ARE ENJOYABLE AND EASY TO UNDERSTAND, WHETHER YOU ARE A NOVICE OR VETERAN CRAFTER.

GETTING STARTED

If you are like me, you probably want to jump right into the projects in this book. Still, there are some basic preparations covered in this section that will make your crafting experience more enjoyable and help your projects look their best. Here you will learn how best to gather materials, prepare your surface, transfer a pattern and make a stencil.

PREPARING YOUR SURFACE

To make your project go smoothly, to achieve the best results and to ensure that your projects continue to look their best, take care to properly prepare your surface before painting or decorating.

CLEAN SURFACES

Always begin your project with a clean surface. For glass and tin surfaces, clean well with a little rubbing alcohol on a paper towel. Let the surface dry completely. Before working on terra-cotta, make sure it is dry and wiped clean of any dirt.

PRIME RAW CANVAS

If you purchase raw canvas to use as a floor cloth, apply a coat of acrylic paint, latex paint or artist's gesso on both sides of the cloth. These primer coats will seal the canvas so that it does not absorb too much paint when stenciled. The primer will also keep the canvas from curling.

SEAL WOOD

To prepare bare wood, sand it with medium, 100-grit sandpaper and wipe it clean of any dust. Then seal it with an acrylic sealer. Pay close attention to knots and dark marks in the wood. If not sealed properly, these areas could come through the basecoat and mar the painted surface. Let the sealant dry completely before applying a basecoat.

PRIME WOOD FOR A MOSAIC

If you're using a wooden surface for a mosaic, first seal the wood and then prime it with a mosaic primer. The primer will help mosaic tiles adhere properly to the wood. You can find mosaic primer wherever mosaic supplies are sold.

APPLYING A PAINT BASECOAT

You will start many of the wood projects in this book by applying a basecoat of acrylic paint. Be sure to sand and seal your wood before you follow the steps below.

1 **APPLY THE FIRST COAT**
After sealing the wood with acrylic sealer, apply a basecoat of acrylic paint using a large flat or basecoating brush. Allow the paint to dry completely.

2 **SAND THE SURFACE**
Once you've applied the basecoat, the moisture in the paint tends to make the wood fibers come out again. Lightly sand the surface with medium, 100-grit sandpaper.

3 **APPLY THE TOPCOAT**
Add a second coat of acrylic paint and let it dry. Now you can decorate your surface.

TRANSFERRING A PATTERN

You'll find the patterns for the projects in this book on pages 116–123. The basics for transferring a pattern to a wood, glass or tin surface are the same. Use translucent tracing paper to trace the pattern from this book. Or use a small light box designed for home crafters and regular paper. If you need to adjust the pattern size, enlarge or reduce the traced design on a photocopier.

You will need masking tape, transfer paper and a tracing or embossing stylus to copy the pattern onto your surface. Choose a waxless and greaseless transfer paper because the marks won't bleed through paint. Blue water-erasable type transfer paper can be wiped away with a damp sponge.

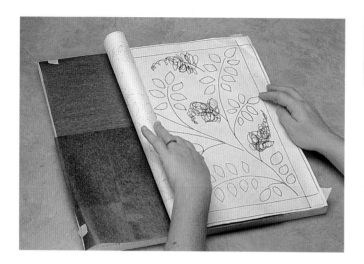

1 POSITION THE TRANSFER PAPER AND PATTERN
Prime or basecoat your surface as needed. Lay the transfer paper face down onto your surface and tape it in place with masking tape. Place your pattern face up on top of the transfer paper and tape it in place.

2 TRACE THE PATTERN
Use a tracing stylus to copy the pattern. Use a light touch and try not to press down on the surface with your hands so you don't make any smudges. If you're just making one project, you can use a pen instead of a stylus, but a pen will make your pattern difficult to reuse.

3 CHECK THE PATTERN AS YOU GO
Carefully lift the pattern and transfer paper occasionally to make sure the pattern is transferring smoothly. Retrace any sections you may have missed.

MAKING AND USING A STENCIL

Making your own stencils is easier than you'd think and much less expensive than precut stencils. You can use freezer paper, Mylar or plastic as a stencil material. Freezer paper is inexpensive and quick and easy to cut, but it's delicate and won't last as long as a Mylar or plastic stencil. However, you can cut two layers of freezer paper at once, so you can make two identical stencils at once. To make your stencils, you will need plastic-coated (not wax-coated) freezer paper, masking tape, a sharp, round-handled craft knife with a no. 11 blade and a self-healing cutting mat. The round handle of the craft knife makes handling much easier and more accurate. Spray adhesive will help hold the finished stencil in place on your project.

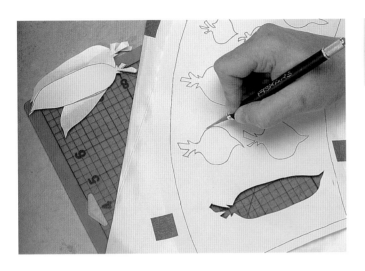

1 CUT THE STENCIL

Transfer the pattern onto plain paper following the instructions on page 10. Place two pieces of freezer paper, both shiny side up, on your work surface. Place the pattern face up on top and tape all three pieces together. Place them on the cutting mat and use a craft knife to cut the stencils. As you cut, rotate the papers so you're always pulling the craft knife toward yourself.

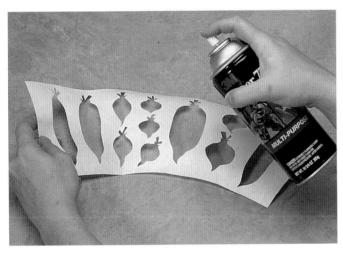

2 COAT WITH SPRAY ADHESIVE

Spray the back—nonshiny side—of the stencil with a spray adhesive and let it dry. If the stencil starts to lose its stickiness, spray it again. Once dry, place the stencil on your surface.

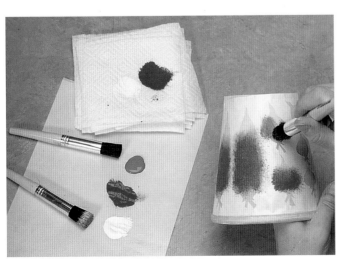

3 USE THE STENCIL

Use a different stencil brush for each color of paint. To load the brush, dip it into the paint and pounce hard on a pile of paper towels to remove the excess paint and work the remaining paint up into the brush.

Place your freezer paper stencil on the surface and apply the paint by holding your brush vertically and pouncing it over the stencil. Make sure you cover all areas, including the edges of the shapes, evenly. If you notice that the paint bleeds under the stencil, you are using too much paint. You should be able to paint many areas before loading the brush again.

BASIC TECHNIQUES

The following pages introduce you to the basic techniques you will need to work with the materials in this book, including polymer clay, paint, wire, metal and pour-on polymer coating. Take the time to review these techniques before you begin, especially if you are trying a product or technique for the first time.

WORKING WITH POLYMER CLAY

Working with polymer clay is an undemanding way to fashion stunning objects for the garden. Proper conditioning, baking and finishing will result in classy projects that friends will not believe you created yourself. Simple household tools are all you need. I prefer soft clay that remains strong and flexible after firing. I like Original Sculpey and Premo! Sculpey polymer clays for the projects in this book.

GENERAL SAFETY

Any surface that comes in contact with polymer clay—the pasta machine, rollers, molds, tile and other surfaces—cannot be used again for food preparation. Make sure your tools are well labeled "for polymer clay use only."

When baking your pieces, make sure the room has good air circulation. Pets and small children are more sensitive to the fumes and should not be in the room during the baking process.

CONDITIONING POLYMER CLAY

Before you begin any polymer clay project, you have to condition the clay. Conditioning makes the polymer clay more pliable and easier to mold, and it makes the clay stronger after it is baked. For large batches of clay, use a pasta machine dedicated to use with clay.

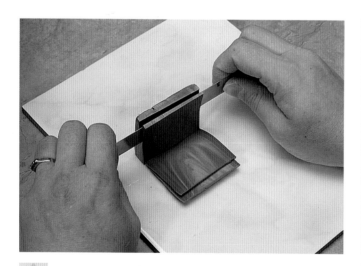

1 CUT THE CLAY INTO SLICES
Start by cutting the clay into thin slices so they'll fit through the pasta machine. A 6" (15 cm) long, thin steel blade, called a polymer clay knife, works best.

2 CONDITION THE CLAY
Run the slices through a pasta machine set to the widest setting. Fold the clay in half and put it through again, fold first. Repeat this process about twenty to twenty-five times to soften and condition the clay. You also can knead the clay with your hands or roll it out with a hand roller until it reaches a good working consistency.

SHAPING POLYMER CLAY

There are a number of ways you can work with polymer clay. Below are some of the common techniques used in this book. I recommend using a large glazed 10" (25 cm) tile as a work surface. You can create your polymer clay pieces on the tile and then bake both the tile and the pieces in the oven.

Using a Decorative Mold
Press polymer clay into flexible molds to create detailed, dimensional motifs. Glue the clay to your project before baking.

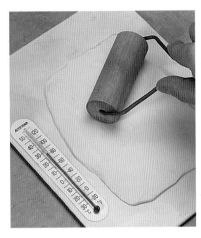

Rolling Clay Flat
A wooden or clear acrylic roller is good for smoothing out thick slabs of polymer clay that can then be cut with a sharp craft knife.

Smoothing Edges
A plastic sculpting knife is helpful for smoothing seams. You also can soften edges with your fingertips.

Adding Texture
Anything can be pressed into polymer clay to add texture. Try rough-edged rocks, leaves, flowers and rubber stamps.

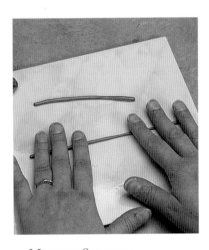

Making Strands
Use your fingertips to roll clay out into thin strands. You can loop and braid these to make embellishments.

Painting Clay
Brush metallic powders onto unbaked clay with a soft brush, or paint the clay with acrylics after it is baked.

BAKING THE CLAY

Bake the finished clay pieces in your home oven or a toaster oven dedicated to crafts. Bake at 275° F (135° C) for approximately fifteen minutes per ¼" (6mm) of thickness. Refer to the manufacturer's instructions for the exact temperature and baking time for the clay you are using. To avoid burning the clay, use a separate oven thermometer to make sure the oven is at the right temperature. It is generally OK to bake the clay a little longer than recommended, but never allow the oven temperature to get hotter than recommended.

WORKING WITH PAINT

Painting with acrylics is an easy and effective way to transform any plain craft surface into something truly your own. Many of the projects in this book include some basic painting. The good news is that you do not need any special skills to paint beautifully. Need to brush up on the basics? The information detailed here will give you a good start.

SELECTING BRUSHES AND PAINTS

Review the materials list at the beginning of each project. Be mindful of the type of paint that is being used in each project and use the proper paint for each particular surface. Outdoor projects often call for weatherproof paint or paint for metal, both of which resist peeling and fading.

Painting is more enjoyable when you use the right brushes for your projects. A large flat or basecoating brush is best for quickly coating a surface. Round and flat brushes in several sizes are good for general painting and detail work. Specialty brushes such as a deer foot stippler or splatter brush make certain paint effects easy to achieve. Finally, a variety of sponges from foam rollers to sea sponges are handy for creating softly blended colors on any surface.

THINNING AND BLENDING PAINTS

Most paint can be brushed, sponged or stenciled directly on your surface. Occasionally, though, you will want to thin or blend the paint first to achieve the best results. Pay attention to the instructions given with each project. Weatherproof and metal paints should be thinned with a clear acrylic medium manufactured to work with that particular paint. Don't thin them with water. When working on fabric, you can add acrylic fabric medium to your paint to make it softer and more permanent. Here are the most common ways paint can be thinned and blended.

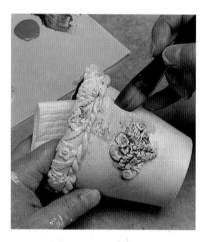

CREATING A WASH
To create a delicate wash for highlights and details, thin ordinary acrylic paint with a bit of water. If you are using weatherproof paint, mix it with clear acrylic medium in a fifty/fifty blend instead.

Green and brown washes are wonderful for antiquing textured surfaces. Wipe off the excess paint with a damp towel.

CREATING A GLAZE
Mix equal amounts of glazing medium and acrylic paint when you want to make colors more transparent. Glazing medium is especially useful when you want to color black-and-white clip art without covering the details.

BLENDING WITH A SPONGE
You can use a sea sponge to create a mossy effect. Dip the sponge into two different colors of paint, then wipe the excess onto a paper towel. Apply the paint with a pouncing action, working the paint in for a soft and natural look.

WORKING WITH WIRE AND METAL

Wire and metal are good choices for garden projects. They are easy to use and stand up well to the elements. Craft stores carry fine gauge craft wire, embossing styluses and thin rolls of embossing metal. Look in your local hardware store to find wire cutters, pliers, copper pipe, pipe connectors and copper cable.

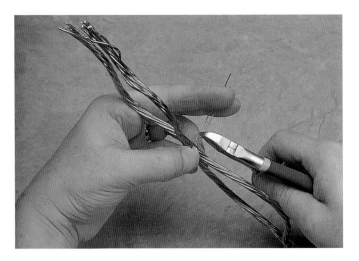

CUTTING WIRE

When cutting wire, try to hold the piece you're removing, as well as the main piece, so it doesn't fly off and injure you or someone close by. If you are unable to hold both ends, point the piece you're cutting off toward the floor so it doesn't fly through the air.

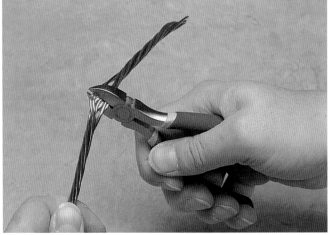

CUTTING COPPER CABLE

For cutting thick, multistrand wire cable, hold the cable with the wire cutters and bend the cable back and forth until metal fatigue breaks the wire cleanly.

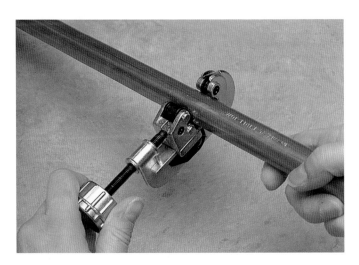

CUTTING PIPE

Use a special pipe cutter to cut copper pipe. Place the pipe in the cutter and rotate the cutter around the pipe as you tighten the wheel to score and cut the pipe. If you do not have a pipe cutter, ask the store where you purchase the pipe to cut it to size.

EMBOSSING METAL FOIL

For embossing thin metal sheeting, place the metal piece face up on a soft foam surface, such as a mouse pad. Press down lightly with an embossing stylus to emboss the metal.

USING A POUR-ON POLYMER COATING

The easiest way to create a thick, clear, high-gloss finish on a project is to use a pourable polymer coating. These plastic coatings can be poured onto a variety of project surfaces and, when cured, provide a thick, permanent, waterproof, high-gloss finish. I use Envirotex Lite pour-on high-gloss finish for the projects in this book. It comes in two parts, a resin and a hardener, and when equal parts are mixed together they react chemically to form the polymer coating.

PREPARATION AND SAFETY

Before you apply the liquid polymer coating to a project, assemble the materials listed at right in a warm, well-ventilated workspace free of dust and safe from pets and small children. Work on a clean, level surface protected with wax or freezer paper. Wear protective gloves and avoid contact with your eyes or skin.

Elevate the item you are coating about 2" (5cm) above the work surface to allow the coating to drip freely off the sides. I like to prop my projects up on several disposable plastic cups. While the coating is still liquid, you can wipe up any accidental drips with rubbing alcohol. Once the coating has cured, you can safely discard the mixing cups, stir sticks and glue brushes in the household trash.

> ### BASIC MATERIALS
>
> - plastic disposable measuring cup (for mixing)
> - wooden stir stick
> - disposable glue brush
> - wax paper or freezer paper
> - clear plastic tape
> - several paper or plastic disposable cups
> - disposable latex gloves
> - heat gun (optional)

MIXING THE TWO-PART RESIN

Proper mixing of the two-part resin is necessary to assure a clean, hard finish without soft spots.

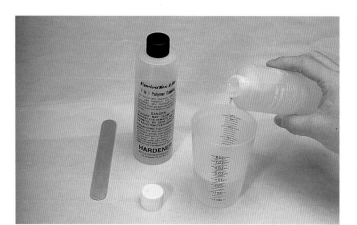

 MEASURE THE RESIN AND HARDENER
Wearing disposable latex gloves, measure the resin and hardener in a single disposable plastic measuring cup. Measure exact amounts by volume. Do not try to guess, or your coating will be soft and sticky. Measure out only the amount you need for the item to be coated, about four ounces (118ml) per square foot (929 square centimeters).

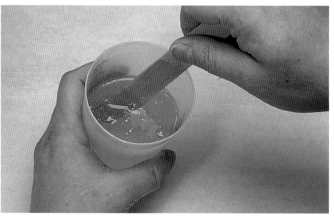

 MIX THE RESIN
Use a wooden stir stick and stir vigorously for two minutes until thoroughly blended. Continually scrape the sides and bottom while mixing to avoid soft or tacky spots on your finished piece. Do not worry about bubbles; they are a sign you are mixing well.

COATING YOUR SURFACE

Follow the steps below to get the best results. Mix the proper amount of polymer coating for your project immediately before pouring it on your surface.

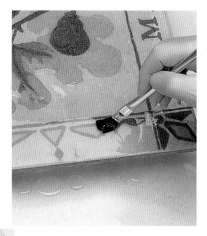

1 TAPE THE PROJECT BOTTOM
Before you pour polymer coating on your project, protect the bottom from excess drips by firmly taping the edges with clear tape.

2 POUR THE RESIN
Elevate your project on paper cups over wax paper and pour the mixed resin onto your project right away. Pour in a circular pattern, starting close to the edge and working toward the center. This will allow the coating to level out.

3 BRUSH THE COATING
Spread the coating where necessary with a glue brush. Be careful not to spread the coating too thin, or the surface will be wavy. You have about twenty-five minutes of working time before the coating starts to set up.

4 ELIMINATE THE AIR BUBBLES
Within ten minutes, air bubbles will rise to the surface. Gently exhale (do not blow) across the surface to get rid of them. The carbon dioxide in your breath will burst any bubbles. On large surfaces, use a heat gun, holding it no closer than three to four inches (8 to 10cm) from the surface.

5 CURE AND CLEAN THE SURFACE
Let the item cure overnight. Envirotex Lite cures to the touch in about twelve hours and cures fully in seventy-two hours. Remove the tape from the bottom of the project and the drips will pop off. Remove remaining drips by sanding them off.

PROTECTING YOUR WORK

Properly protecting your finished work will help your project last for years of enjoyment. Here are the most important tips for making sure your projects will look their best.

On painted projects that you plan to display outdoors, use acrylic paints designed for outdoor use. Unlike ordinary acrylic paints, weatherproof acrylic paints (such as Metal Paint and Patio Paint) need no protective topcoat of varnish. They are designed to be resistant to peeling and fading.

Découpaged projects or those that have been painted with ordinary acrylic paint should be finished with a protective water-based varnish coating. Two or more coats of a clear water-based varnish will keep découpaged papers from peeling off and paint from chipping. Acrylic paint manufacturers provide varnishes that work with their paint lines. To finish a painted floor cloth, I prefer Varathane Elite Diamond Finish. This water-based varnish is designed to protect against heavy floor traffic and can be found in hardware stores. It also also works well on polymer clay.

APPLYING A PROTECTIVE FINISH

Coat your painted and découpaged projects with several thin coats of clear, water-based varnish by following these directions.

1 SEAL PAPERS AND DRIED FLOWERS
Before adding the finishing varnish coats to découpaged surfaces, coat any flowers or handmade papers with a fine layer of thin-bodied white glue. This helps to protect dried flowers from excess moisture and seals paper pieces that otherwise might change color after a few coats of varnish. Let the glue dry completely clear before adding the finishing varnish coat.

2 PREVENT PAINTS FROM BLEEDING
Paint pens and permanent markers can run and bleed if not protected before you apply a water-based varnish. Apply a light coat of spray varnish before you brush on any additional finish. Shake the can well and spray from 12" (30cm) away with broad, even strokes to completely cover the piece with a thin protective layer. Let this coat dry completely before adding the final varnish coat.

3 APPLY THE VARNISH
Roll the varnish container instead of shaking it to minimize bubbles on your finished piece. Pour the varnish into a small disposable bowl to prevent the entire supply from being contaminated. Apply the varnish with a large soft brush in slow, thin coats.
Let each coat dry before adding another layer. Apply at least two coats. The more thin coats you apply, the tougher the surface will be.

WATERPROOFING A POT

You can waterproof a terra-cotta pot by coating the inside with a high-gloss, pour-on polymer coating. A waterproof pot makes a beautiful vase for fresh cut flowers and contains water that could leak from potted plants.

1 POUR ON THE POLYMER COATING
Tape over the drainage hole in the bottom of the pot. Tip the pot and pour freshly mixed resin down the sides. Rotate the pot as you pour to reach the entire inside surface.

2 SMOOTH WITH A BRUSH
Use a glue brush to help coat the inside up to, but not over, the top edge. Set the pot aside to cure.

CARING FOR YOUR PROJECTS

Take the time to properly care for your projects by following the general guidelines below. If you are giving the piece as a gift, include the care instructions.

PAINTED AND VARNISHED SURFACES

To clean up dirt or spills, do not immerse these items in water. Simply wipe them clean with a damp cloth.

FABRIC

Use special care when washing hand-painted clothing, such as the stenciled pear apron on page 22. Wash painted fabric in the washing machine on the gentle cycle with a soap cleaner, not a detergent. Hang to dry.

To care for a varnished canvas floor cloth, simply wipe with a damp sponge. If it develops tough stains or scuff marks, gently sand until the mark is gone with a fine grade (200-grit) sandpaper. Then revarnish the floor cloth with at least two coats of heavy-duty varnish. Coat the back with a brush-on, nonskid rug backing.

PROJECTS INTENDED FOR OUTDOOR USE

Mosaic tabletops, polymer clay pieces and tiles coated with polymer coating are sturdy and hold up quite well in the outdoors. However, it is best to bring them indoors during harsh winters. Do not let water sit on top of the mosaic table for extended periods of time. Keep painted objects out of direct sunlight, which can eventually fade the colors.

Polish glass mosaic tiles by rubbing on a light coat of olive oil. Maintain high-gloss polymer coatings with a yearly coating of furniture polish or a carnauba-based car wax. Apply a thin coat with a rag. When dry, buff the piece briskly with a soft cloth.

The Bountiful Garden

Ah, the joys of late summer when the days are long, gardens overflow with fresh vegetables, and fruit trees are full of ripe fruit ready to pick. It makes you want to celebrate all of nature's bounty. The good news is you don't have to have a green thumb to bring the beauty of golden pears, green onions, hearty cabbage, tomatoes and carrots into your home. This section offers you five creative projects that will bring the vibrant colors, forms and textures of fruits and vegetables to life.

Learn how to adorn a garden apron with juicy pears, brighten pots with stenciled vegetable motifs, découpage a seed-saving box, paint a colorful floor cloth and make a garden journal for recording all your discoveries in the garden. Make these projects as a year-round reminder of nature's bounty, or give them as practical gifts to garden-loving friends and family.

A PLAIN MUSLIN GARDEN APRON IS THE PERFECT CANVAS FOR SOME BRIGHTLY STENCILED BRANCHES LOADED WITH RIPE, JUICY PEARS. STENCILING IS A FUN AND EASY WAY TO DECORATE FABRIC. PUT THE PEAR BRANCH PATTERNS—THE BRANCHES, TWIGS, LEAVES AND FRUIT—TOGETHER TO "GROW" YOUR DESIGN AS BIG OR SMALL AS YOU LIKE ACROSS THE APRON FRONT. TO ADD EXTRA INTEREST, WRITE THE MANY NAMES OF PEAR VARIETIES WITH A PERMANENT FABRIC MARKER.

Stenciled PEAR APRON

BEFORE YOU BEGIN

❧ *When stenciling on fabric, add **acrylic fabric medium** to the paint. Fabric medium allows the paint to penetrate the fibers of the material, making the stenciled design more permanent. The medium also makes the paint more translucent for easier shading and a lighter appearance. Place a quarter-sized puddle of acrylic fabric medium beside each acrylic color on your palette. Mix into a 50/50 blend on your palette with the stencil brush.*

YOU WILL NEED

- blank muslin apron

- photocopies of the pear and pear name patterns (page 117)

- freezer paper

- masking tape

- cutting mat

- craft knife

- spray adhesive

- acrylic paints (DecoArt Americana):
  Golden Straw, Antique Gold,
  Hauser Medium Green, Plantation Pine,
  Antique Maroon, Deep Burgundy,
  Burnt Sienna

- acrylic fabric medium

- stencil brushes: ½" (13mm) and 1" (25mm)

- disappearing ink marking pen
  (erasable fabric marker)

- black permanent fabric marker

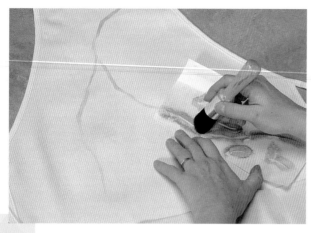

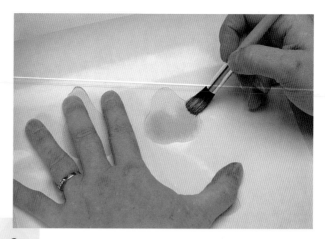

1 STENCIL THE BRANCHES
Make freezer paper stencils of each pattern follow-ing the instructions on page 11. Prepare your palette by mixing each color with an equal amount of acrylic fabric medium.

    Load a 1" (25mm) stencil brush with Burnt Sienna and very lightly stencil on the main branches. Move the stencil around, adding branches and twigs in a simple arrangement on the apron. These branches will be your guide for placing the pears and leaves.

2 STENCIL THE PEARS
With a ½" (13mm) stencil brush, stencil on the pears, applying Golden Straw paint over the center of each pear shape. Following the law of gravity, the large, ripe pears should hang straight down from the branches. The smaller, unripe pears can hang at slight angles.

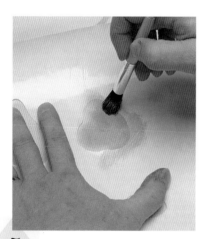

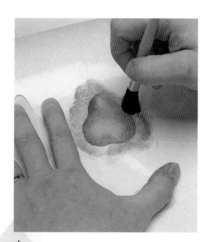

3 ADD SHADING
Add additional depth to each pear by shading the edges and top with Antique Gold.

4 ADD DEEPER COLORS
Add more color by stencil-ing in Deep Burgundy and Antique Maroon around the contours of the pear. Keep the shading rounded to emphasize the plump shape of the fruit. Add a little Hauser Medium Green to the small pears to suggest various stages of ripeness.

5 STENCIL THE LEAVES
Use a 1" (25mm) stencil brush and Hauser Medium Green to add leaves along the branches. Shade the edges with Plantation Pine. Lift the stencil periodically to check your progress. Where one leaf overlaps a pear or another leaf, allow the leaf color to fade. Add more leaves until you are satisfied with the design.

6 ◈ DARKEN THE BRANCHES

With the ½" (13mm) stencil brush, go back over the branches with a deeper Burnt Sienna. Using the same color, add veins to the leaves, and attach the pears to the branches with stems.

7 ◈ ADD FINAL TOUCHES

Add a touch of Burnt Sienna to the base of each pear with the ½" (13mm) stencil brush to indicate the blossom end. Stencil Antique Gold highlights onto some of the leaves.

8 ◈ WRITE THE PEAR NAMES

With the disappearing ink pen, write *Pears* at the top of the apron. Add a variety of pear names to the pockets. When you are pleased with the placement of each name, go over the lettering with a permanent pen. The temporary marks eventually will fade away.

The Finished Apron

FILL THE POCKETS OF YOUR GARDEN APRON WITH PRUNING SHEARS, SEED PACKETS AND OTHER HANDY GARDEN ITEMS. USE SPECIAL CARE WHEN WASHING THE APRON. WASH IT IN THE WASHING MACHINE ON THE GENTLE CYCLE WITH A SOAP CLEANER, NOT A DETERGENT. HANG TO DRY.

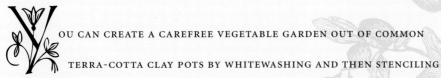

YOU CAN CREATE A CAREFREE VEGETABLE GARDEN OUT OF COMMON TERRA-COTTA CLAY POTS BY WHITEWASHING AND THEN STENCILING THEM WITH COLORFUL VEGETABLE MOTIFS. WHAT MAKES THESE POTS UNIQUE ARE THE DETAILS CARVED WITH A HANDHELD ROTARY TOOL. ENLARGE OR REDUCE THE VEGETABLE PATTERNS TO MAKE THE STENCILS FIT ANY SIZE POT.

Etched VEGETABLE POTS

BEFORE YOU BEGIN

❧ *A **rotary tool** is a versatile power tool with interchangeable heads for grinding, drilling, buffing and polishing. Attach a cone grinding bit for a fun and easy-to-use etching tool.*

❧ ***White Lightning** is a sealer and white stain in one. It creates a semitransparent white-wash effect when applied to wood or terra-cotta. You can purchase White Lightning in craft stores.*

YOU WILL NEED

- 5½" (14cm) tall, 5" (13cm) in diameter terra-cotta clay pot(s)

- White Lightning varnish (or clear acrylic varnish tinted with white acrylic paint)

- brushes: 1" (25mm) flat brush for basecoating, ¾" (19mm) stencil brush

- radish patterns (page 120)

- freezer paper

- masking tape

- cutting mat

- craft knife

- spray adhesive

- acrylic paints (DecoArt Americana): Hauser Medium Green, Cherry Red, Titanium (Snow) White

- paper towels

- handheld electric rotary tool with a ⅜" (10mm), 120-grit cone grinding bit

- medium (100-grit) sandpaper

- clear varnish

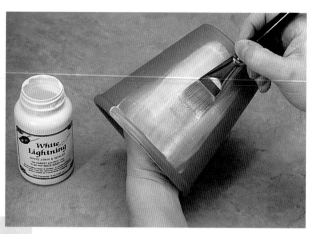

1 CREATE THE POT STENCIL

To make an arc template to fit your clay pot, roll the pot over a large sheet of paper and trace the arc at the base of the pot. Without lifting the pot, roll it back and trace along the top. Transfer the radish pot pattern to the paper, then follow the instructions on page 11 to make a freezer paper stencil.

2 PAINT THE POT

Use a basecoating brush to whitewash the pot with White Lightning. When the pot is completely dry, wrap the sides of the pot with your stencil.

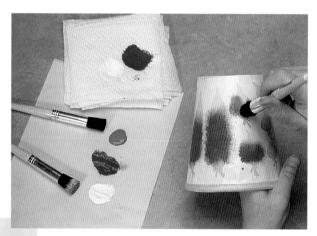

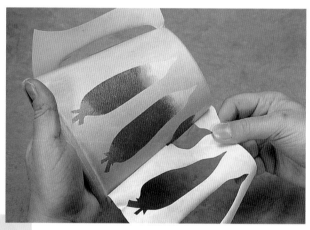

3 STENCIL THE RADISHES

Work Titanium (Snow) White paint into a ¾" (19mm) stencil brush and pat off excess paint onto a paper towel. Pounce the acrylic paint through the stencil openings along the bottom of the radishes. Next, stencil the bodies of the radishes in Cherry Red and the tops in Hauser Medium Green.

4 REMOVE THE STENCIL

Carefully peel off the stencil and set the pot aside to dry.

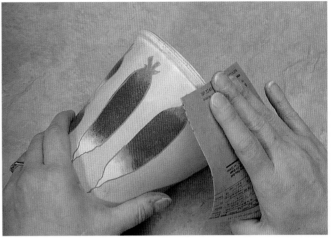

5 ETCH AROUND THE BORDERS
Using the rotary tool with a ⅜" (10mm) 120-grit cone grinding bit, etch in the lines around the vegetables, adding detail to the design. If you've never used a rotary tool before, practice on a plain pot first. This is easier than it looks.

6 SAND AND SEAL THE POT
Sand the edges of the pot to create a distressed look and apply a finishing varnish coat following the instructions on page 18.

◆ **FUN VARIATIONS** ◆

Decorate additional pots with peas and eggplants for a colorful trio of vegetable motifs. Use the vegetable patterns on page 120 and the following colors of paint:

𝒫EAS: OLIVE GREEN, HAUSER MEDIUM GREEN, HOLLY GREEN

𝓔GGPLANTS: HAUSER MEDIUM GREEN, ROYAL PURPLE, SNOW WHITE

The Finished Pot

THE ETCHED LINES CREATED BY THE ROTARY TOOL ADD CHARACTER AND DIMENSION TO THE RADISHES. IF YOU CHOOSE A RIMMED POT, TRY ETCHING THE NAME OF THE VEGETABLES AROUND THE RIM.

ARVESTING, SAVING AND SHARING SEEDS IS A GREAT FAMILY HOBBY THAT IS ENJOYING RENEWED RECOGNITION. HERE IS THE PERFECT PROJECT TO INSPIRE YOUR OWN SEED GATHERING. THIS ANTIQUED WOODEN BOX IS DECORATED WITH TINTED, DÉCOUPAGED VEGETABLE MOTIFS. THE PAINTED WOOD FAUX FINISH, PAIRED WITH THE OLD VEGETABLE ENGRAVINGS, GIVE THIS BOX AN HEIRLOOM APPEARANCE. THE EMBOSSED METAL LABEL AND LITTLE TIN CONTAINERS FINISH OFF THIS GARDEN OFFERING.

Rustic SEED BOX

BEFORE YOU BEGIN

❧ **Watchmaker's tins** *were originally made to store gems, watch movements and jeweler's findings. These glass-topped aluminum containers are ideal for saving seeds. You can find them at craft stores or via specialty suppliers.*

❧ **Glazing medium** *is formulated to be mixed with acrylic colors to make a "glaze" or a more translucent paint. The mix can be varied to achieve different intensities, but a general 50/50 blend works just fine.*

❧ *To glue down paper, use* **découpage glue** *or white glue that is thin enough to spread easily with a foam brush yet strong enough to hold paper down. It is important that the glue dries crystal clear, as you'll be applying it as a topcoat to seal and protect.*

❧ **Aluminum embossing metal** *is sold in rolled sheets in craft stores.*

YOU WILL NEED

- 10¾" x 7¼" x 2⅓" (27cm x 18cm x 6cm) hinged wooden box
- white paraffin or beeswax
- acrylic brushes: 1" (25mm) flat for basecoating, no. 4 flat, no. 6 round, 1" (25mm) foam brush
- acrylic paints (DecoArt Americana): Khaki Tan, Desert Sand, Titanium (Snow) White, Golden Straw, Hauser Medium Green, Jade Green, Deep Burgundy, Georgia Clay, Royal Purple
- medium (100-grit) sandpaper
- copyright-free clip art of vegetable motifs (Dover Pictorial Archive Series)
- clear varnish
- glazing medium
- scissors with a fine point

- découpage glue
- craft knife
- sheet of 22-gauge aluminum embossing metal
- soft foam pad for embossing, such as a mouse pad
- 1" (25mm) circle template
- embossing stylus
- silicone-based glue
- metal card or label frame
- old garden book pages, photocopied with brown toner (optional)
- watchmaker's tins (the seed box comfortably holds six 2" (5cm), eight 1½" (4cm) and five 1¼" (3cm) containers)
- adhesive labels (optional)

1 WAX SECTIONS OF THE BOX

You'll give this box a well-worn, rustic appearance by sanding through several layers of paint. To begin the process, rub a piece of white wax onto the box in areas that would show natural wear, such as the edges and patches on the top and sides. The wax works as a resist, so sanding off the paint in the distressing process will be easier.

2 APPLY THE FIRST TWO LAYERS OF PAINT

Brush on a single coat of Khaki Tan paint with the basecoating brush and let it dry. Rub more wax onto the box then brush on a coat of Desert Sand paint. Let the box dry completely.

3 ADD THE FINAL COAT AND SAND

Rub more wax onto the box and brush on a coat of Titanium (Snow) White paint. Let the paint dry. Then sand the surface with medium (100-grit) sandpaper to reveal various layers of underlying paint. Set the box aside while you prepare the vegetable motifs.

4 SEAL THE VEGETABLE MOTIFS
Brush a clear varnish coat onto several photocopied images of vegetable clip art. This will seal the paper and prepare it for the glazes. Let the images dry completely before proceeding.

5 GLAZE THE MOTIFS WITH COLOR
Prepare your paint palette with Hauser Medium Green, Jade Green, Golden Straw, Deep Burgundy, Georgia Clay and Royal Purple acrylic paints and a puddle of glazing medium beside each color. Mix equal amounts of each paint and glazing medium on the palette to create transparent tints.

Use the round and flat brushes to apply the glazed paint. Don't worry about going over the outside lines, as you will be cutting out the images. If you can't see the image details under the tinted glaze, you are not using enough glazing medium in your mixture. Let the motifs dry completely.

6 PASTE THE MOTIFS ON THE BOX
Cut out the vegetable motifs with scissors. Using découpage glue and a foam brush, paste the images onto the box top and sides. Then brush glue over the pasted images to protect. Cut through any images that overlap the seam of the box lid with a craft knife. Set the box aside to dry.

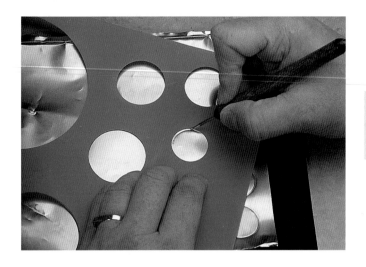

7 TRACE METAL CIRCLES FOR THE BOX CORNERS
Place a sheet of aluminum embossing metal on a foam pad. Use a circle template and embossing stylus to trace eight 1" (3cm) circles onto the metal sheet.

8 FOLD AND TRIM THE BOX CORNERS
Cut out the circles and fold to create four equal-sized wedges. Unfold each circle and cut one of the quarter pieces out.

9 GLUE THE METAL CORNERS TO THE BOX
Wrap the metal circles around the box corners along the metal folds. Placing the seams along the side edges, glue the metal into place with silicone-based glue. Rub any sharp edges down with the edge of a closed pair of scissors.

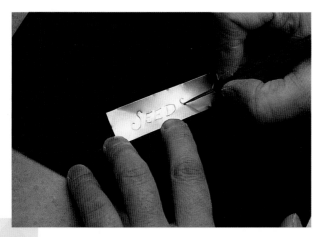

10 CREATE THE BOX LABEL

Cut out a 1" x 3" (3cm x 8cm) piece of aluminum embossing metal. Place it on a foam pad and use an embossing tool to lightly write the word *Seeds* on one side of the metal.

11 EMBOSS THE BACK OF THE LABEL

Flip the metal piece over. Using the lightly embossed lines as a guide, firmly emboss the reversed word with the embossing tool.

12 FURTHER HIGHLIGHT THE FRONT

Flip the metal label over again and make the embossed image stand out even more by tracing around the embossed letters to create a cleaner and deeper image.

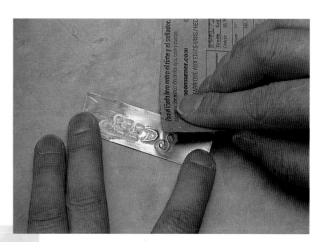

13 PAINT THE LABEL

Paint over the top of the label with white acrylic paint, and let it dry. Then sand the surface to reveal the lettering.

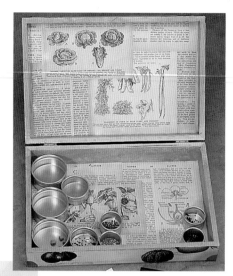

14 ATTACH THE LABEL TO THE BOX
Glue the seed label on the box top with silicone-based glue and frame it with a metal label frame.

15 DECORATE THE INSIDE
Follow the instructions on page 18 to protect your box with a couple coats of clear varnish. Line the inside of the lid and bottom of the box with copied pages from a garden manual using découpage glue and a finishing coat of varnish. Add an assortment of watchmaker's tins and adhesive labels so you will be ready to mark the date and variety of your saved seeds.

The Finished Seed Box

THE CREATIVE PROCESS OF MAKING YOUR SEED BOX AND COLLECTING SEEDS FROM YOUR GARDEN ARE BOTH REWARDING AND EDUCATIONAL FOR THE WHOLE FAMILY.

IF YOU HAVE NEVER COLLECTED SEEDS, THE FOLLOWING PAGE OFFERS HELPFUL TIPS FOR SUCCESSFULLY PRESERVING SEEDS FROM YOUR GARDEN.

HOW TO DRY AND STORE SEEDS

Saving seeds is a deeply satisfying activity. Exchange your favorite seeds with friends or preserve heirloom varieties not found in stores. The rewards are well worth the effort.

Save seeds from the biggest and best plants in your garden to promote seed diversity and assure that you preserve the varieties that perform best in your own local climate. Saving the seeds from the best plants allows you to grow bigger plants with larger and tastier crop yields over a period of years. For example, squash cross-pollinates so freely you may end up with a completely new and improved variety. Here is the basic technique, followed by tips for some of the easiest vegetable seeds to preserve.

1 REMOVE AND DRY THE SEEDS

To preserve seeds from fleshy vegetables, such as this acorn squash, cut the fully ripened vegetable open and scrape the seeds out with a spoon. Remove any excess pulp and set the seeds on a paper towel to dry completely.

2 STORE AND LABEL THE SEEDS

Once dry, place the seeds in the containers and label the tins with the name of the variety and the harvest date. Make sure the containers and seeds are completely dry or the seeds will rot. Carefully store the seeds in a cool, dry place. Some saved seeds can last up to five years if stored properly.

SEEDS EASY TO PRESERVE

Beans and Peas	Allow the pods to dry brown before harvesting. If frost threatens, pull up the whole plant and hang in a cool, dry location to complete the drying.
Corn	Harvest the corn after the husks have turned brown. Pull back the husks to expose the cobs and complete the drying in a cool, dry location. Twist the dried ears to allow kernels to fall off the cob.
Cucumbers and Tomatoes	Let the fruit ripen completely on the vine. Cucumbers and tomatoes should turn a golden color. Slice the fruit open and scrape out the seeds with a spoon. Place them in a jar with a little water in a warm location for two to three days. A beneficial fungus that helps protect the seeds from diseases and removes their jellylike coating will form. Rinse the seeds well and place on paper towels until dry.
Onions, Lettuce, Radishes and Spinach	Let the plants flower and wait until they have gone to seed. Carefully cut down the ripe seed stalks and place them carefully in brown paper bags to avoid losing the seeds. This method is good for saving many flower seeds as well. Let the stalks dry upside down in the open paper bags. The seeds should fall out with a good shake of the dried stalks. You may need to winnow the seeds, which means to remove the plant debris.
Melons and Squash	Harvest seeds from ripe and ready-to-eat fruit. Leave summer squash on the vine until it is fully ripe and the shell hardens. Rinse the seeds clean if necessary and dry on paper towels.

Brighten a garden shed or kitchen floor with this hand-painted floor cloth. You'll start with a primed canvas floor cloth and stencil it with vegetable motifs in a patchwork pattern. The stencil technique is fast and fun with basic shading and no complicated overlays. Add the word welcome to greet visitors or add a fun garden saying. Add bold line borders with a black paint pen to give the motifs a nonstenciled appearance.

Vegetable Patch FLOOR CLOTH

BEFORE YOU BEGIN

❧ *This project uses two kinds of **paint rollers.** The 3⁄8" (10mm) pile roller is a soft, fuzzy roller that quickly applies a thick layer of paint. The dense foam roller rolls out a thin, even layer of paint. Its firmness leaves sharp edges and does not bleed under your tape borders.*

❧ *You can use raw artist's **canvas** or preprimed canvas, which is available at fine art supply stores. Use white acrylic paint or gesso to prime both sides of a nonprimed canvas. Then hem it to prevent fraying. I used Kreative Kanvas from Kunin Felt. It is constructed with a durable plastic core and covered on both sides with smooth, white, fray-proof fabric. I like to prime both sides to prevent the corners from curling and to keep it from absorbing too much paint.*

YOU WILL NEED

- 25" x 33" (64cm x 84cm) primed canvas floor cloth

- acrylic paints (DecoArt Americana): Hauser Medium Green, Toffee, Khaki Tan, Shale Green, Olive Green, Hauser Light Green, Country Red, Royal Purple, Titanium (Snow) White, Georgia Clay, Plantation Pine, Deep Burgundy

- paint roller with 3⁄8" (10mm) pile and paint tray for basecoating

- yard stick and ruler

- chalk pencil

- 1⁄4" (6mm) and 1" (3cm) wide low-tack masking tape

- craft knife

- cutting mat

- 4" (10cm) dense, foam roller, for painting the panels

- vegetable and garden phrase patterns (pages 118–119)

- freezer paper

- brushes: assorted stencil brushes from 1⁄2" (13mm) to 1" (25mm), no. 1 round; large, soft brush

- black paint pens, fine- and medium-point

- matte spray varnish

- water-based acrylic finish

- brush-on rubber rug backing

FLOORCLOTH LAYOUT

Use this diagram and the Color Palette below as a guide to paint the floor cloth. Basecoat colors are listed in parentheses. The entire cloth measures 25" x 33" (64cm x 84cm). The wide margins are 1" (3cm) and the narrow margins are ¼" (6mm).

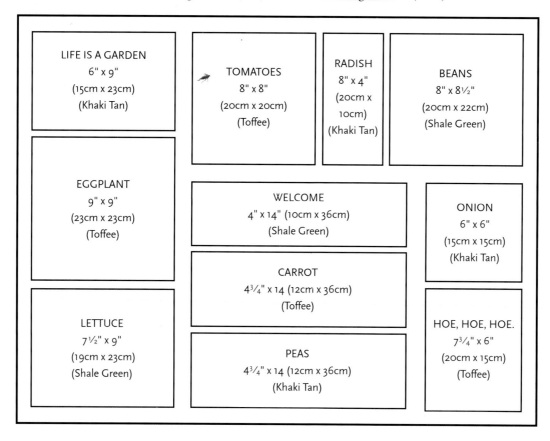

LIFE IS A GARDEN 6" x 9" (15cm x 23cm) (Khaki Tan)	**TOMATOES** 8" x 8" (20cm x 20cm) (Toffee)	**RADISH** 8" x 4" (20cm x 10cm) (Khaki Tan)	**BEANS** 8" x 8½" (20cm x 22cm) (Shale Green)
EGGPLANT 9" x 9" (23cm x 23cm) (Toffee)	**WELCOME** 4" x 14" (10cm x 36cm) (Shale Green)		**ONION** 6" x 6" (15cm x 15cm) (Khaki Tan)
	CARROT 4¾" x 14 (12cm x 36cm) (Toffee)		
LETTUCE 7½" x 9" (19cm x 23cm) (Shale Green)	**PEAS** 4¾" x 14 (12cm x 36cm) (Khaki Tan)		**HOE, HOE, HOE.** 7¾" x 6" (20cm x 15cm) (Toffee)

COLOR PALETTE

Use this color palette as a guide to paint the panels in the floor cloth.

BASECOAT: Hauser Medium Green

PANELS: Toffee, Khaki Tan, Shale Green

SEEDLINGS: Olive Green, Hauser Light Green, Hauser Medium Green

LADYBUGS: Olive Green, Country Red

EGGPLANTS: Hauser Medium Green, Royal Purple, Titanium (Snow) White highlight

LETTUCE: Olive Green, Hauser Light Green, Hauser Medium Green

TOMATOES: Country Red, Hauser Medium Green, Titanium (Snow) White highlight

CARROTS: Georgia Clay, Hauser Medium Green

PEA PODS: Hauser Light Green, Hauser Medium Green, Olive Green

RADISHES: Country Red, Titanium (Snow) White, Hauser Medium Green

BEANS: Hauser Medium Green, Plantation Pine

ONION: Deep Burgundy, Toffee, Hauser Medium Green

1 BASECOAT THE CANVAS

Cut the primed canvas to 25" x 33" (64cm x 84cm), making sure the corners are perfectly square. Use a ⅜" (10mm) pile paint roller and Hauser Medium Green paint to basecoat the floor cloth.

2 MARK THE PANELS

Follow the diagram on the previous page to measure and mark lines on the floor cloth with a chalk pencil and yard stick. Make sure all the corners are square and even.

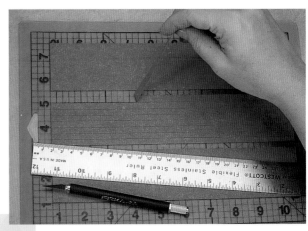

3 MASK THE BORDERS

Mask the border and the wide margins between the panels with 1" (3cm) low-tack masking tape. Mask the narrow margins with ¼" (6mm) masking tape. If you can't find ¼" (6mm) masking tape, place 1" (3cm) strips of tape onto a cutting board and cut them to size with a ruler and craft knife.

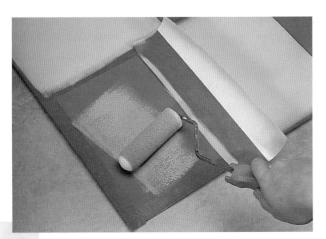

4 PAINT THE PANELS

Using the dense foam roller, paint the panels according to the diagram on page 40. Tape freezer paper over adjacent panels when painting a panel near narrow margins.

For the best results, use a different roller for each color and store the rollers in separate plastic bags so they don't dry out. This way, you don't need to wash the roller and wait for it to dry between each color, and you can quickly apply additional coats as soon as the first ones are dry.

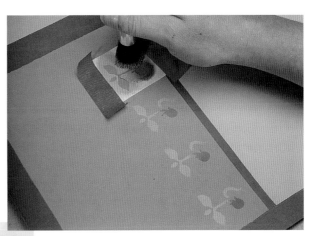

5 STENCIL THE SEEDLINGS

Trace or copy the vegetable patterns and follow the instructions on page 11 to make a freezer paper stencil for each vegetable.

Remove the masking tape and stencil a row of seedlings in the top left panel, one at a time. Using separate ½" (6mm) stencil brushes for each color, stencil the seed pod in Olive Green and the sprout in Hauser Medium Green. Blend the colors together where they meet. Lift the stencil and repeat the motif across the bottom of the panel.

6 STENCIL THE EGGPLANTS
In the left middle panel stencil two eggplants. Stencil the top of each eggplant with Hauser Medium Green and the fruit in Royal Purple. Don't worry about blending the colors. The detail lines you'll add later will give a more realistic look.

7 ADD OTHER VEGGIES
Using the photo on page 43 as a guide, stencil the other vegetables and ladybugs in the same manner. Use the Color Palette on page 40 for color suggestions. As you finish each vegetable, carefully peel off the stencil to prevent it from tearing.

8 ADD HIGHLIGHTS
Add highlights to the eggplants and tomatoes in Titanium (Snow) White with the ½" (6mm) stencil brush, pouncing it on the fruit in a little circle. Add small highlights to the seed sprouts with a no. 1 round brush.

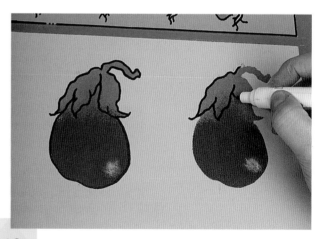

9 TRACE ON THE LETTERING
Photocopy the garden phrase patterns. Trace the lettering onto the floor cloth with transfer paper and a tracing stylus. Fill in the letters with a medium-point black paint pen.

10 ADD DETAILS TO THE VEGETABLES
Outline each vegetable with a fine-point black paint pen. Add details to the vegetables, giving an individual charm to each one: Add veins to the leaves, ridges to the carrots and onions and curls and vines to the pea pods. You can paint these freehand or trace the details lightly with a pencil before going over them with the paint pen. Draw spots and antennae on the ladybugs and add dotted lines behind some of the ladybugs to show their paths.

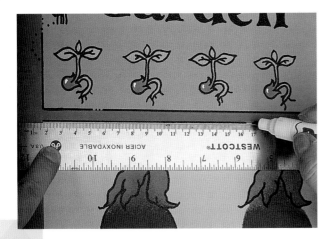

11 OUTLINE THE PANELS

Use a ruler and a fine-point black paint pen to trace around the panels. Use dots instead of a solid line in some spots to add interest. Draw a black border around the entire floor cloth.

12 SEAL THE PAINT, THEN VARNISH

Spray the entire floor cloth with a light coat of matte spray and let it dry. This will seal the paint-penned lines so they don't bleed when you apply the varnish. Then brush on several coats of water-based acrylic varnish with a large, soft brush to protect the floorcloth from wear.

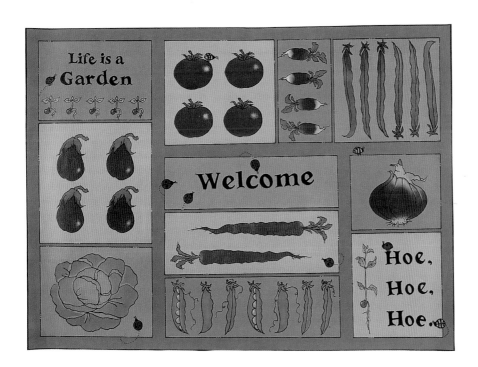

13 ADD A BACKING

Brush on a liquid rubber rug backing with a large, soft brush to make the floor cloth nonskid.

The Finished Floor Cloth

LET THE FLOOR CLOTH CURE FOR AT LEAST TEN DAYS BEFORE USING IT. TO CARE FOR THE FLOOR CLOTH, SIMPLY WIPE WITH A DAMP SPONGE. FOR TOUGH STAINS OR SCUFF MARKS, GENTLY SAND WITH A FINE GRADE (200-GRIT) SANDPAPER UNTIL THE MARK IS GONE. THEN REVARNISH WITH AT LEAST TWO COATS.

So many happy discoveries occur in the garden, and keeping a garden journal is one of the best ways to make sure those memories never fade. This handmade garden journal uses a simple Japanese bookbinding technique that doesn't require fancy supplies or equipment. The journal is adorned with natural handmade papers, a pressed skeleton leaf and twig accents. Finish it with a clever technique for creating a three-dimensional pea pod motif.

Handmade GARDEN JOURNAL

BEFORE YOU BEGIN

❧ *You can find* **decorative and hand-made papers** *in art and craft supply stores. Soft, flexible Japanese paper works best for the cover. Also visit your local photocopy store for a selection of papers appropriate for the inside. Ask an employee to cut the paper to size.*

❧ **Fusible adhesive,** *also called fusible webbing, is available in the fabric department of your craft store. For bookbinding, Steam-A-Seam 2, with its slightly sticky surface, is a favorite. It adheres temporarily until a hot iron creates a permanent, stronger bond.*

YOU WILL NEED

- four pieces of mat board or heavy cardboard
- cutting mat
- craft knife
- ruler with cork backing
- glue stick
- three pieces of handmade tan paper
- 12" x 20" (31cm x 51cm) piece of taupe cotton fabric
- 12" x 20" (31cm x 51cm) piece of paper-backed fusible adhesive
- iron
- rotary cutter
- two pieces of decorative garden print paper
- stack of naturally colored, text weight paper
- two large rubber bands
- thick scrap of wood
- drill with ⅛" (3mm) bit

- large needle
- natural raffia
- 5" (13cm) twig
- piece of handmade green paper
- two pressed skeleton leaves
- wax paper
- brushes: 1" (25mm) foam brush, glue brush, no. 4 flat
- thick white craft glue
- piece of card stock or thin cardboard
- 10" (25cm) square glazed ceramic tile for a work surface
- white polymer clay
- polymer clay roller
- pea pod pattern (page 117)
- plastic sculpting knife
- acrylic paint (Americana): Jade Green

1 CUT THE MAT BOARD

Place the mat boards on the cutting mat and measure and mark two 7" x 5" (18cm x 13cm) book covers and two 1" x 5" (3cm x 13cm) hinges. Make sure the board is square to the grid marks on your cutting mat so you can cut straight lines. Hold the ruler down firmly with your noncutting hand and draw the knife blade toward you with a firm, strong stroke. You may need to make a few strokes to cut through the board cleanly.

2 GLUE ON THE COVERS

Cut two 9" x 7" (23cm x 18cm) pieces of tan hand-made paper. Using a glue stick, apply a layer of glue over the entire back of a piece of tan paper. Place a mat board cover in the center of the glued paper and fold the corners over at a 45° angle.

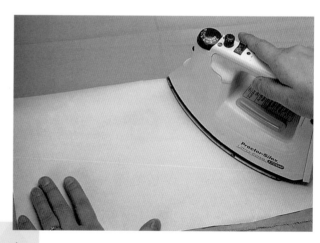

3 FOLD THE FLAPS

Fold the side flaps over and rub them firmly to adhere the paper to the board. Turn the cover over and rub the front to smooth.

4 APPLY FUSIBLE ADHESIVE TO THE FABRIC

Repeat steps 2 and 3 to cover the second board. Use an iron to lightly fuse the taupe fabric to the fusible adhesive. Cut two 4" x 8 " (10cm x 20cm) pieces from this fused piece using a rotary cutter, ruler and cutting mat. These pieces will cover the spine and hinges of the book. Fold each fabric piece in half lengthwise to mark the center.

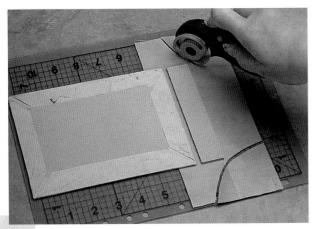

5   POSITION THE COVERS ON THE FABRIC

Remove the backing from one piece of fabric. Along the center of the fabric, place one of the smaller pieces of mat board that you cut. Position the cover $\frac{3}{16}$" (5mm) away from the hinge, right side down. Make sure all pieces are square to the grids on the cutting mat. Trim away the outer corners of the fabric with a rotary cutter. Cut curved lines that come within about $\frac{1}{4}$" (6mm) of the corners of the small piece of mat board.

6   IRON THE SIDE FLAPS

Fold the side flaps so they overlap both pieces of mat board and iron them lightly to hold the fabric in place. Press down the small overlapping sections of fabric at each corner with the point of the iron.

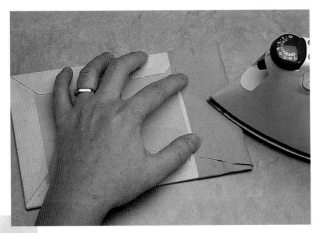

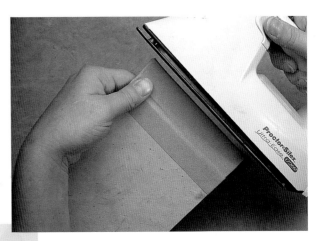

7   IRON THE END FLAP

Iron down the top flap. Then turn the cover over and iron the fabric on the front by running the point of the iron over the space between the hinge and cover and then moving outward.

8   PRESS THE EDGES

Make sure the fabric is well adhered by ironing over all the fabric surfaces, including the edges of the cover. Repeat steps 4 through 8 to attach the other hinge and cover.

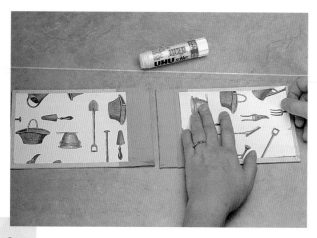

9 ADD THE END PAPERS

Cut two 6½" x 4½" (17cm x 11cm) pieces from the decorative garden print paper. Adhere these decorative end papers to the insides of the covers with a glue stick.

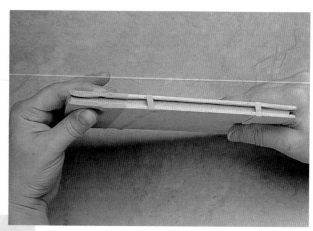

10 PLACE THE PAGES BETWEEN THE COVERS

Trim a ¼" (6mm) stack of natural colored text-weight paper to 4½" x 8" (11cm x 20cm). Center the stack between the covers, aligning it exactly with the end papers at the nonspine side of the covers. The pages should extend past the hinge on the other end. Carefully wrap large rubber bands around the book to hold the pages firmly in place.

11 MARK AND DRILL THE HOLES

In the middle of the hinge, measure and mark three binding holes at 1⅛"(3cm), 2½" (6cm) and 3⅞" (10cm) from the top. Place the book over a thick piece of scrap wood. Drill ⅛" (3mm) wide holes through all the pages and covers.

12 BIND THE BOOK WITH RAFFIA

Place the twig beside the binding holes. Thread a large needle with 25" (64cm) of raffia and follow the binding diagram on page 49 to bind the book together. Try to avoid piercing the raffia with the needle as you sew so you don't weaken or even split the binding. Finish the raffia binding with a bow in the front center.

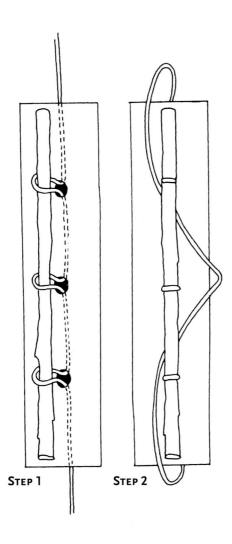

STEP 1 STEP 2

BINDING DIAGRAM

Leave a 6" (15cm) length of raffia at the beginning hole. Then bring both ends from behind the book and pull them under the twig. Finish by tying a bow with the loose ends.

13 DECORATE THE COVER

Tear a 3¼" x 3¾" (8cm x 10cm) piece of green hand-made paper. Glue it onto the front cover with a glue stick. Place two skeleton leaves on a sheet of wax paper. Use a pouncing motion to apply craft glue to the back of each leaf with a foam brush. Position the leaves on the front cover and let dry.

14 CUT THE PEA SHAPES

Use a clay roller to roll conditioned white polymer clay onto a glazed tile. Roll the clay to ⅛" (3mm) thick. Make card stock templates of the pea pod patterns. Place the templates on the clay and cut out the pea pod shapes with a craft knife.

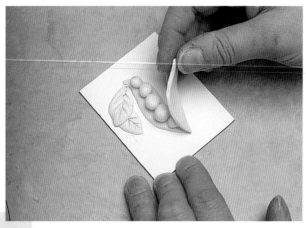

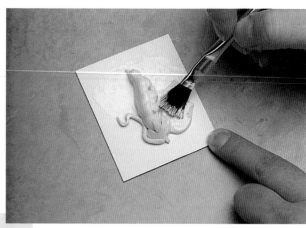

15 ASSEMBLE THE PEA POD

Cut a piece of thin cardboard to 2¼" x 2¾" (6cm x 7cm). Position the small clay leaves and the bottom layer of the pea pod on the cardboard. Press veins into the leaves with a plastic sculpting knife. Make the peas by rolling small balls of polymer clay in the palm of your hand. Position the peas on the pea pod and place the top layer of the pod over the peas and a little to one side.

16 BAKE THE POD, THEN COAT WITH GLUE

Add the coiled vine and calyx. Place the cardboard panel with the finished pea pod on the ceramic tile and bake following the instructions on page 13. Let it cool. Glue the pod onto the panel and coat the entire surface with craft glue.

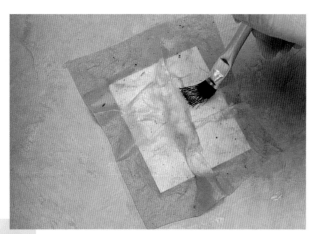

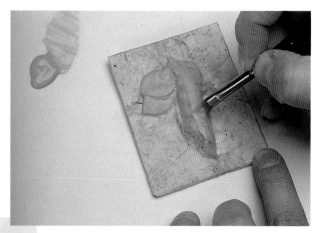

17 COVER THE PEA POD WITH PAPER

Cut the third piece of handmade tan paper to 3½" x 4½" (9cm x 11cm), and dip it quickly into clean water. Lay it over the pod. Push the paper into the contours of the pea pod with the glue brush and some craft glue. Fold the flaps around the back of the panel and leave it overnight to dry completely.

18 PAINT THE PEA POD

Thin a bit of Jade Green paint with water and apply a thin wash over the pea pod with a no. 4 flat brush. Let it dry. Then glue the panel and pea pod to the front of the journal with craft glue.

19 DECORATE THE TITLE PAGE
Embellish the title page with a label and images cut from the decorative garden paper.

The Finished Journal

YOUR GARDEN JOURNAL IS READY TO RECORD YOUR FAVORITE VARIETIES OF FLOWERS OR VEGETABLES. SEE THE BOX BELOW FOR CREATIVE IDEAS TO HELP YOU MAKE THE MOST OF YOUR JOURNALING EXPERIENCE. IF YOU PREFER FLOWERS TO VEGETABLES, REPLACE THE PEA POD ON THE FRONT COVER WITH A SUNFLOWER MOTIF.

HOW TO KEEP A GARDEN JOURNAL

USE YOUR GARDEN JOURNAL TO RECORD YOUR GARDEN'S PROGRESS—ACHIEVEMENTS AND CHANGES— OR YOUR THOUGHTS ON A DREAM GARDEN. SEPARATE THE JOURNAL INTO THE MONTHS OF THE YEAR, GIVING THE SPRING AND SUMMER MORE ROOM THAN THE SLOWER GROWING MONTHS IN THE WINTER. THE GREATEST REWARD IN KEEPING A JOURNAL IS NOT SIMPLY OWNING A RECORD OF YOUR ACHIEVEMENTS BUT LEARNING FROM YOUR EXPERIENCES. A GARDEN JOURNAL CAN INCLUDE ANY OF THESE ITEMS:

- Photographs of your garden; before and after shots are very rewarding.
- Maps to remind you where you planted bulbs and seasonal plants
- Lists of items you planted and when and where you bought them
- Pictures, botanical names and growing instructions from seed packets and plant tags
- Clippings from garden magazines and newspapers

- Harvest yields from your vegetable garden
- Chore calendar; list dates for planting, checking soil type, sowing seeds, transplanting into the garden, fertilizing schedules and the best times for pruning, mulching, etc.
- Birds and other wildlife observed in the garden
- Future garden plans

Old World Tuscany

The projects in this section will remind you of quiet, walled court-yards paved in warm-toned marble, or perhaps a secluded, sun drenched garden retreat under a deep blue Mediterranean sky. Each project is an invitation to relax and create something special to grace your kitchen, patio or windowsill.

Begin your Mediterranean garden with terra-cotta containers aged with a beautiful patina. Fill them with fragrant herbs such as opal basil, lemon balm or flowering thyme. Learn a sand mosaic technique for accenting plain ceramic tiles with classical fruit motifs and Latin sayings. Maybe you're looking for something dramatic: create a colorful mosaic table in deep greens, purples and blues. The bright glass tiles will stir up visions of spiraling rosemary bushes and fragrant citrus trees. Finally, greet guests with a weathered welcome sign that looks as if it were carved from stone or learn how to embellish a large flower vase with elegant gold ivy leaves made of gilded polymer clay.

T HESE TERRA-COTTA POTS MIMIC EXPENSIVE DECORATIVE POTS FROM
FINE GARDEN AND GIFT SHOPS. THE DECORATIVE MOTIFS ON THE
POTS ARE MADE OF POLYMER CLAY THAT IS PAINTED AND ANTIQUED TO
APPEAR WORN AND OLD. CHOOSE FROM TWO EMBELLISHING TECHNIQUES:
PRESS POLYMER CLAY INTO A MOLD TO CREATE A DECORATIVE MOTIF, OR
IMPRESS A DESIGN INTO THE CLAY WITH RUBBER STAMPS. COAT THE INSIDE OF
THE POTS WITH A THICK, POUR-ON POLYMER COATING TO MAKE WATERTIGHT
VASES, OR LEAVE THEM PLAIN FOR PLANTING.

Tuscan FLOWERPOTS

BEFORE YOU BEGIN

❧ *Look in the fabric department of a craft store to find a* **tracing wheel** *for tracing patterns onto fabrics. The wheels come in a variety of sizes and create a decorative, evenly spaced dotted line on polymer clay.*

❧ *This project uses* **weatherproof acrylic paints** *specially formulated for outdoor use. I used Patio Paint.*

❧ **Polymer clay molds,** *or push molds, are flexible plastic molds used for shaping polymer clay into decorative borders and motifs. Soap and candy molds also work; just remember that once you use them for polymer clay, you cannot use them for food preparation.*

YOU WILL NEED

- terra-cotta pots in various sizes from 3½" to 5" (9cm to 13cm) in diameter
- 10" (25cm) glazed ceramic tile as a work surface
- polymer clay molds
- brushes: soft brush, glue brush, 1" (25mm) flat
- cornstarch
- terra-cotta polymer clay
- polymer clay knife
- white glue
- weatherproof acrylic paints (DecoArt Patio Paint): Daisy Cream, Fern Green, Woodland Brown
- natural sea sponge
- glazing medium
- paper towel
- pasta machine
- ruler
- craft knife
- rubber stamps
- tracing wheel

1 PREPARE THE POLYMER CLAY MOLD

Find a mold with a leafy border pattern suitable for the rim of your pot. Brush a light coating of cornstarch into the mold with a soft brush to prevent the clay from sticking. After you remove the polymer clay from the mold, you can brush off any excess powder with a clean soft brush.

2 FILL THE MOLD WITH POLYMER CLAY

Press some conditioned polymer clay into the mold. (For tips on working with polymer clay, see pages 12–13.) To fill deep areas of the mold, form the clay into a cone shape and apply pressure. Level off excess clay from the top of the mold with a polymer clay knife to create a flat backing.

3 BRUSH GLUE ONTO THE POLYMER CLAY

Brush glue on the back of the motif while it is still in the mold.

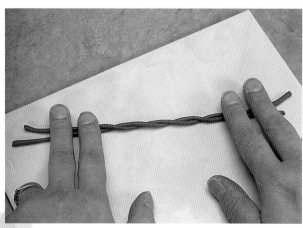

4 DECORATE THE RIM
Remove the clay from the mold. Wrap the molded clay piece around the rim of the pot. Repeat steps 1 through 4 until you've covered the rim. Gently blend the seams together with your fingertips.

5 MAKE A BRAIDED BORDER
Wind two long strands of polymer clay together. Brush one side with glue and wrap it around the pot just below the first border. Then use an accent mold to make two decorative motifs for the sides of the pot. Glue them onto the pot and let dry.

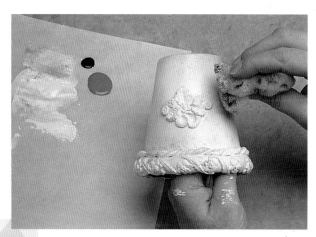

6 BAKE AND BASECOAT THE POT
Once all the glue is dry, bake the pot following the instructions on page 13. After it has cooled, basecoat the pot with Daisy Cream acrylic paint and a 1" (25mm) brush. Apply two coats for complete coverage, making sure to cover all the deep details.

7 ADD SOME SHADING
Mix Fern Green, Woodland Brown and some Daisy Cream to keep the shade soft. Sponge the pot with a natural sea sponge loaded with this mixture.

8 ANTIQUE THE POT
Create a glaze by making a 50/50 mixture of Woodland Brown paint and glazing medium. Apply washes over the pot, working on a small section at a time, and push the paint into the deep details.

9 REMOVE THE EXCESS PAINT
Continuing to work on small areas, wipe off the excess paint immediately with a damp towel to create an antiqued look. If the effect is too subtle, add another layer of glaze and wipe again. Repeat on all areas of the pot. Set the finished pot aside to dry.

The Finished Pot

YOU CAN CREATE INTERESTING VARIATIONS ON THIS BASIC DESIGN BY USING MOLDS WITH DIFFERENT DESIGNS. IF YOU'D LIKE TO WATERPROOF YOUR POT FOR INDOOR USE, FOLLOW THE INSTRUCTIONS ON PAGE 19.

◆ CREATIVE VARIATION ◆

Try imprinting unbaked polymer clay with rubber stamps (see page 59). The design possibilities are endless. This rustic pot looks wonderful planted with herbs and perched on a windowsill or sunny table.

Create the pretty harlequin variation on page 58 by pressing rubber stamps into the clay.

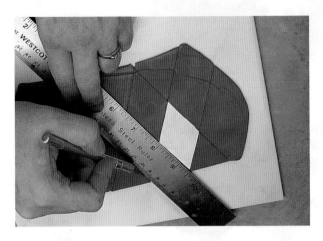

 ### 1 CUT CLAY DIAMONDS
Roll some conditioned polymer clay through the pasta machine on the thickest setting and place it on the glazed tile. Cut twelve 2" x 3" (5cm x 8cm) diamonds using a ruler and a craft knife. Also cut a long strip of clay to wrap around the rim of the pot.

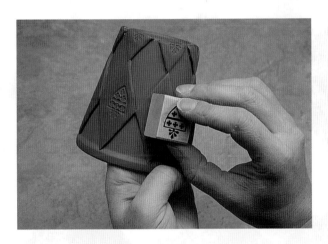

 ### 2 GLUE AND STAMP THE CLAY
Apply a thin layer of glue to the back of each piece of clay, and then position it on the pot. Trim any edges that hang over the edge of the pot with the polymer clay knife. Let the glue dry. Then carefully stamp the center of each diamond with a rubber stamp. Soften the edge of each stamped area with your finger to better adhere the clay to the pot and finish the rough edges.

 ### 3 EMBELLISH WITH A TRACING WHEEL
Add a stippled design around the diamonds and the rim with a tracing wheel. Follow steps 6 through 9 on pages 57-58 to bake, paint, antique and finish the pot.

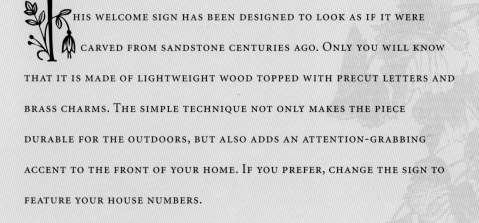

THIS WELCOME SIGN HAS BEEN DESIGNED TO LOOK AS IF IT WERE CARVED FROM SANDSTONE CENTURIES AGO. ONLY YOU WILL KNOW THAT IT IS MADE OF LIGHTWEIGHT WOOD TOPPED WITH PRECUT LETTERS AND BRASS CHARMS. THE SIMPLE TECHNIQUE NOT ONLY MAKES THE PIECE DURABLE FOR THE OUTDOORS, BUT ALSO ADDS AN ATTENTION-GRABBING ACCENT TO THE FRONT OF YOUR HOME. IF YOU PREFER, CHANGE THE SIGN TO FEATURE YOUR HOUSE NUMBERS.

Mossy STONE WELCOME SIGN

BEFORE YOU BEGIN

❧ *This project uses* **weatherproof acrylic paints** *that are especially formulated for outdoor use. There are several brands available; I used Patio Paint.*

❧ *A* **pour-on polymer coating** *is a thick, high-gloss coating made by mixing a two-part resin. Once hardened, it forms a strong, waterproof coating on your project.*

YOU WILL NEED

- 11" x 14" (28cm x 36cm) oval wood plaque
- pencil
- white craft glue
- 1½" (4cm) tall self-adhesive wood letters to spell "welcome"
- brass acorn charms
- carved wooden motifs
- 40" (102cm) of thick rope
- brushes: 1" (25mm) flat for basecoating, glue brush
- weatherproof acrylic paints (DecoArt Patio Paint): Antique Mum, Cloud White, Fern Green, Light Sage Green, Golden Honey
- clear plastic tape
- paper cups
- freezer paper
- plastic gloves
- pour-on polymer coating
- plastic cups for mixing
- stir sticks
- beige sand
- natural sea sponge
- flat applicator sponge
- sawtooth picture hangar

1 ATTACH THE LETTERS AND EMBELLISHMENTS

Lightly draw guidelines for placement of the letters on the plaque. Remove the protective backing from the letters and adhere them in place. If your letters don't have an adhesive backing, glue them on with craft glue. Attach the carved wooden accents, acorn charms and rope with craft glue. Let the plaque dry completely.

2 BASECOAT THE PLAQUE

Basecoat the entire plaque with Antique Mum acrylic paint to seal the surface and make all the accents a uniform color. Let the paint dry completely.

3 APPLY A POLYMER COATING

Apply tape on the back of the plaque, along the edge, to protect it from drips. Place the plaque on several small paper cups over a sheet of freezer paper so the coating will drip neatly off the edges.

Put on plastic gloves and follow the instructions on page 16 to prepare the polymer coating, but instead of pouring it on, brush on a thin coating with a glue brush. Pouring would result in a thick layer that will hide the lettering and accent details.

4 POUR SAND ON THE PLAQUE

When the entire surface is covered with the polymer coating, cover the plaque with beige sand by pouring it out of a plastic cup. Set it aside to cure. Do not tip off the excess sand at this time.

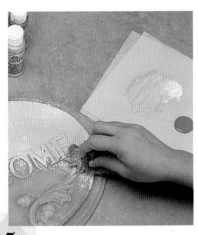  

5 PAINT THE PLAQUE

After the coating has set completely, tip the plaque to remove the excess sand. Remove the tape and drips of resin from the back. With a natural sea sponge, apply a coat of Antique Mum and Cloud White. Load the sponge by picking up one color and then the next. When you dab the sponge on the plaque, the colors will mix softly.

6 ADD SHADING

While the plaque is still wet, sponge Fern Green, Light Sage Green and Golden Honey in selected areas to imitate an old, mossy appearance.

7 ACCENT THE LETTERS

With a flat sponge, add some Golden Honey over the letters to add contrast to the design. When the plaque is dry, paint the back with Antique Mum to seal the wood.

CREATIVE VARIATION

Try this garden compass variation. Glue wooden letters, rope and decorative accents to the bottom of a large terra-cotta flowerpot base. Create the glossy surface by pouring another layer of polymer coating over the finished piece.

The Finished Welcome Sign

ADD A SAWTOOTH PICTURE HANGER TO THE BACK OF THE PLAQUE AND HANG IT PROUDLY TO WELCOME FRIENDS INTO YOUR GARDEN.

BREATHE NEW LIFE INTO A PLAIN GLASS VASE BY ACCENTING IT WITH A RICH GOLD FILIGREE OF NATURAL IVY LEAVES AND CURLING TENDRILS. IMPRINT FRESH LEAVES INTO THE POLYMER CLAY, AND THEN APPLY THE CLAY TO THE VASE. TRY MAKING BRONZED OAK LEAVES, SILVER MAGNOLIA LEAVES OR COPPER MAPLE LEAVES, OR LET LEAVES FROM YOUR OWN GARDEN INSPIRE YOU.

Ivy LEAF VASE

BEFORE YOU BEGIN

❧ **Metallic powders** *are loose powdered pigments available at art and craft stores in a variety of metallic and iridescent colors. I like Pearl-Ex Powdered Pigments. Brush the powders onto unbaked polymer clay to give it a gilded appearance.*

YOU WILL NEED

- 10" (25cm) tall rounded glass vase that fits into your home oven with at least 2" (5cm) of clearance from the heat source and oven walls
- 10" (25cm) glazed ceramic tile as a work surface
- gold metallic polymer clay
- polymer clay knife
- pasta machine
- fresh ivy leaves (or other leaves with a deep vein pattern)
- craft knife
- brushes: glue brush, soft brush
- white craft glue
- plastic sculpting knife
- tracing wheel
- metallic powders (Pearl-Ex): Brilliant Gold, Aztec Gold, Antique Gold
- clear varnish (optional)

1 PRESS IVY LEAVES INTO THE POLYMER CLAY

Cut the stems off of several leaves of various sizes. Condition several sheets of gold polymer clay following the instructions on page 12. Set the pasta machine to the thickest setting. Place the ivy leaves onto a sheet of conditioned clay and roll them through the pasta machine to press the leaf patterns into the clay.

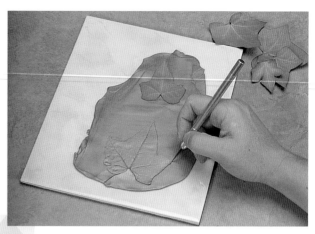

2 CUT OUT THE CLAY LEAVES

Place the polymer clay sheet with the pressed ivy motifs onto a glazed tile. Carefully remove the leaves. Cut out each ivy leaf shape with a craft knife. Press and cut about twelve leaves in all.

3 GLUE THE LEAVES TO THE VASE

Brush craft glue onto the backs of the leaf shapes and wait until the glue tacks up a bit. Then gently press the leaves around the vase in a pleasing arrangement. I limited my design to the middle of the vase.

4 CREATE THE IVY VINES

Roll out long, thin strands of polymer clay. Slightly flatten them and brush on a thin layer of glue. Glue the coils to the vase as stems and curly tendrils.

5   ADD THE LEAF BUDS

Roll tiny amounts of clay in your hand and pinch them to create small teardrop shapes. Apply a thin layer of glue to each bud and add them to the ends of the stems and tendrils. After the glue has set a bit, add a central vein to the small buds with a plastic sculpting knife. Use a tracing wheel to embellish the vines.

6   DECORATE THE RIMS

Run another piece of clay through the pasta machine at the widest setting. Cut it into ½" (13mm) bands with a polymer clay knife. Brush on a thin layer of glue and add these bands to the top and bottom rims of the vase. Smooth the seams with a plastic sculpting knife. Decorate the edges of the bands with the tracing wheel.

7   EMBELLISH THE LEAVES

Use your fingertips to soften and finish the edges of the leaves so they look more natural. Brush metallic powders onto all the clay motifs with a soft brush, alternating the three shades of gold. Then follow the baking instructions on page 13. Turn off the oven and let the vase cool before removing it from the oven.

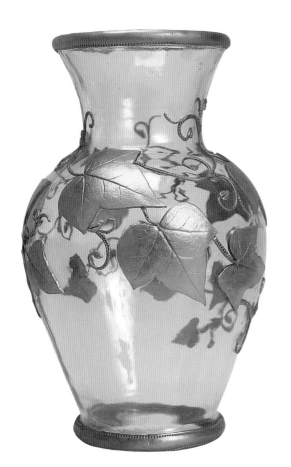

The Finished Vase

IF YOU USE YOUR FINISHED VASE TO HOLD FRESH FLOWERS, COAT THE CLAY WITH CLEAR, WATER-BASED VARNISH TO PREVENT THE POWDER FROM RUBBING OFF. VARNISH ONLY THE POLYMER CLAY AREAS, NOT THE GLASS. TO CLEAN, DO NOT IMMERSE THE VASE IN WATER. SIMPLY WIPE IT CLEAN WITH A DAMP CLOTH.

These tiles look like they might have adorned an ancient Roman courtyard. Create the fine detail with an easy sand mosaic technique that resists fading. Coat the designs with a thick polymer to make them stand up to the outside elements in the garden. The four fruit motifs—grapes, lemons, figs and pears—are simple yet classic. Decorate the borders with these familiar Latin sayings: ut amens ama (to be loved, love). festina lente (hurry slowly), o diem praeclarum (oh, what a beautiful day) and vade in pace (go in peace).

Sand MOSAIC TILES

BEFORE YOU BEGIN

❧ **Colored sand** *is fade-resistant and available in many hues. For even more choices, you can mix different colors together to create new colors. I use sand from Sandtastik.*

❧ *Use* **Matte exterior spray varnish** *to give your finished project a matte finish instead of a high gloss. Make sure you get a high quality exterior spray so it lasts outdoors.*

YOU WILL NEED

- 12" (30cm) ceramic floor tile in a light, neutral color
- fig pattern and lettering (page 122)
- masking tape
- transfer paper
- tracing stylus or pen
- brushes: no. 4 round, glue brush
- thin-bodied white glue
- colored sand (Sandtastik): Brick, Tan, Purple, Green, Blue and Brown
- clear plastic tape
- freezer paper
- paper cups
- plastic gloves
- pour-on polymer coating
- plastic cup for mixing
- stir sticks
- heat gun (optional)
- matte exterior spray varnish (optional)
- fine (600- to 1500-grit) sanding pads (optional)

1 GLUE THE STEMS

Photocopy the fig pattern and transfer it to the ceramic tile following the instructions on page 10. Place the tile on a flat surface over a sheet of freezer paper. Paint white glue over the leaf veins with a no. 4 round brush.

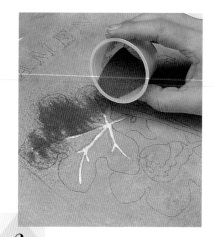

2 SPRINKLE SAND ON THE GLUE

Sprinkle Brick sand onto the glue right away, before the glue starts to dry. Work on small areas and glue only one sand color at a time.

3 POUR OFF THE EXCESS SAND

Tip the tile and let the excess sand fall onto the freezer paper. Funnel the excess sand back into the original container.

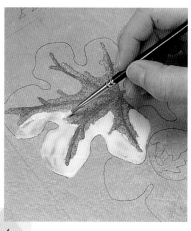

4 ADD MORE SAND

Paint glue over the inner parts of the leaves and cover with a mix of Green and Brick sand. Tip off the excess. Repeat the gluing and sanding for the rest of the leaf. Apply Green near the center, shifting to a mixture of Tan and Green and finishing with Tan near the leaf tips and for the background leaves. It's OK to start a new area without waiting for the previous area to dry.

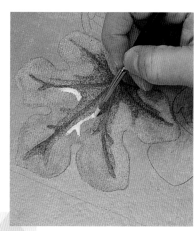

5 LAYER MORE COLOR

Repeat the process over already sanded areas to add further shading. Create a few smaller stems with a mixture of Brick and Brown sand. The pattern is only a start. Add more detail or shading if you wish.

6 FINISH THE DESIGN

Apply glue and sand to the fruit and border. Use Brick and Tan sand individually for the lettering and borders. Use the following colors or mixtures for the figs: Tan, Purple + Tan, Purple, Blue + Purple, Brick and Brick + Purple. The glue will dry clear, so wait for it to dry and then add any finishing touches. Handle the tile carefully. Rough handling can scrape the sand off.

7 COAT THE TILE WITH A POLYMER FINISH
When the glue has dried completely, follow the instructions on pages 16–17 to coat the tile with a thick, waterproof polymer coating.

The Finished Tile

YOU CAN CREATE A MATTE FINISH ON THE TILE BY SPRAYING IT WITH MATTE EXTERIOR SPRAY VARNISH, OR YOU CAN WET THE SURFACE AND SAND IT WITH FINE SANDING PADS MADE ESPECIALLY FOR DÉCOUPAGE WORK. THE WET SANDING TAKES MORE EFFORT, BUT THE RESULTS ARE MORE PERMANENT. BUFF THE TILES WITH CARNAUBA WAX (CAR WAX) ONCE A YEAR TO KEEP THEM LOOKING THEIR BEST.

Mounting Your Tiles

To create stepping stones, mount your tiles onto concrete. Use a stepping stone with a smooth, clean, dry surface and firmly fix it into the ground, or pour new concrete and let it cure for six weeks. Then spread exterior tile adhesive onto the stone or concrete with a notched trowel. Lay the tile on top and firmly weight it down until completely dry.

◆ F R U I T   V A R I A T I O N S ◆

Create more tiles to go with your fig tile. Copy the pear, lemon and grape patterns from pages 122 and 123. Use the sand palettes below to decorate the tiles. Borrow the lettering, border, leaf and stem colors from the tile you just made.

PEARS: TAN, PEACH + TAN , PEACH, BRICK + PEACH, BRICK, BRICK + BROWN

LEMONS: YELLOW, YELLOW + TAN, TAN, BRICK + TAN, BRICK, BRICK + BROWN

GRAPES: TAN, PURPLE + TAN, PURPLE, BRICK + PURPLE, BRICK, BRICK + BROWN

OSAICS HAVE A LONG AND RICH HISTORY. THE ANCIENT
EGYPTIANS, ROMANS, GREEKS AND PRE-COLUMBIANS USED THIS
DECORATIVE TECHNIQUE TO EMBELLISH FURNITURE, BUILDINGS AND HOMES.
THIS MOSAIC TABLE LOOKS LIKE AN ELABORATE WORK OF ART, YET IT USES
STRAIGHTFORWARD, EASY-TO-LEARN TECHNIQUES. THE TILES ARE READILY
AVAILABLE AND EASY TO CUT. YOU'LL ENJOY MAKING THIS TABLE AS MUCH AS
YOU'LL ENJOY LOOKING AT IT AS IT BRIGHTENS YOUR PATIO OR GARDEN.

Mosaic GARDEN TABLE

BEFORE YOU BEGIN

❧ **Vitreous mosaic tiles,** *or tesserae,
are uniform square glass tiles with beveled
edges and ridges on one side for better
bonding. I used Mosaic Mercantile tiles.*

❧ **Sanded grout** *is mosaic grout for heavy
or outdoor use. Look for it in powdered
form at hardware and tile shops.*

❧ *The best* **tile cutters,** *or "nippers," are
made with tungsten-carbide tipped blades
that cut glass tile without shattering. Buy
them where glass mosaic tiles are sold.
Regular tile cutters also work well and are
available at hardware and tile stores.*

❧ *Use a* **grout applicator spatula,** *a
plastic trowel, to apply grout. A* **tile
adhesive applicator** *has toothed edges
that apply ridged lines of adhesive.*

❧ *A* **mosaic sponge/float** *is a sponge
with a smooth rubber float on one side for
smoothing and removing excess grout.*

YOU WILL NEED

◆ 16" x 16" x ¾" (41cm x 41cm x
19mm) plywood base

◆ ¾" (19mm) tesserae (Mosaic
Mercantile): 150 Smoke tiles,
75 Clover tiles, 50 each of
Pansy and Indigo, 30 Glacier
tiles, 25 each of Pale Olive,
Jade and Dew

◆ safety goggles

◆ tile cutters

◆ small broom

◆ large flat brush for basecoating

◆ mosaic primer

◆ mosaic pattern (page 116)

◆ masking tape

◆ transfer paper

◆ tracing stylus

◆ paper cups

◆ glass tile adhesive

◆ tile adhesive applicator

◆ wooden craft sticks

◆ plastic mixing tub

◆ 1-lb. (454g) bag of
sanded grout

◆ grout applicator spatula

◆ mosaic sponge/float

◆ large bucket of clean water

◆ olive oil

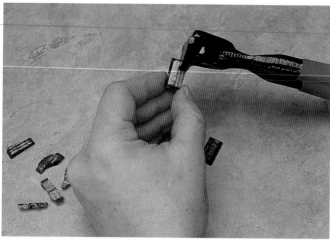

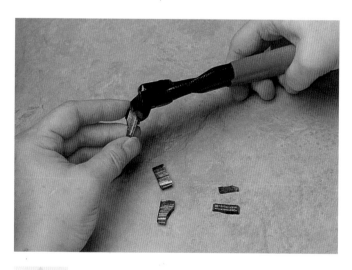

1 **CUT THE STEMS**

Cut the Clover tiles in half along the ridges on the back of the tile. Wear safety goggles when cutting and frequently sweep the tiny glass shards into the trash bin with a broom to keep the area safe.

2 **CUT THINNER PIECES**

Cut each half piece again into a thinner piece. Each original tile will yield three or four stem shapes. Cut about 70 stems.

3 **SHAPE THE STEMS**

Don't worry if some are cut lopsided; just nip off the thicker side to make curved stem pieces. Also don't worry if they don't all look the same. Nature's petals and leaves are all different.

4 **CUT THE LEAVES**

Use the Pale Olive, Jade and Clover tiles for the base. Each tile will make one leaf shape. Cut seven to ten leaves per cluster in the design. Nip the opposite corners off each tile. If a tile breaks in half, just make a smaller leaf by rounding off the sharp corners.

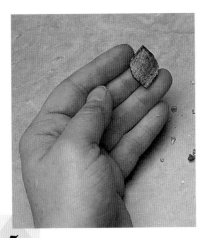

5 · ROUND THE EDGES
Round the edges by nipping with tile cutters to create the leaf shape.

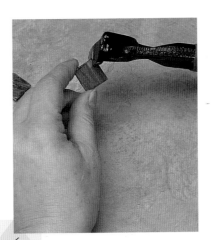

6 · CUT THE FLOWER PETALS
Use the Dew, Indigo and Pansy tiles for the petals. Each tile will make two petal shapes. Cut fifteen to eighteen petals per flower, mixing the colors as you go. Make the first cut on the diagonal, cutting the tile into two triangular pieces. Some will even break on a curve, perfect for petals. Save any extra pieces, even small ones, to fill in spaces in your mosaic as needed.

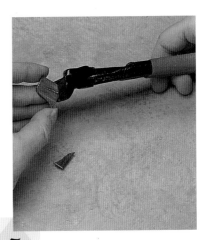

7 · ROUND THE CORNERS
Nip one edge off each triangle to round off the sharp point.

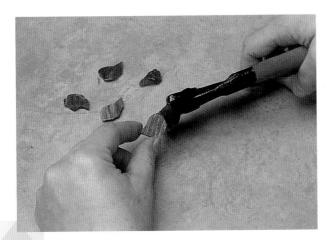

8 · SHAPE THE PETAL
Continue to nip at the square angles to soften the lines of the edges and create petal shapes.

9 · CUT SMALLER SQUARES
Use a full bag of about 150 Smoke tiles for the background. Each tile will make four smaller, square tiles. Cut each tile in half along the ridges as you did in step 1. Then cut the half piece again to make a ³⁄₁₆" (5mm) square piece. Remember, they don't have to be perfect squares, so you can cut lots of pieces quickly.

10 PREPARE THE SURFACE

Prime the plywood on all sides with the mosaic primer and basecoating brush. Use two coats to completely seal and prepare the board for the adhesive and insure that the board will not warp or split in wet weather. Set the board aside to dry completely. Enlarge the pattern and follow the instructions on page 10 to transfer the pattern to the plywood.

11 APPLY THE EDGE TILES

Elevate the plywood using paper cups. Apply glass tile adhesive to a small section of the side edge with a notched tile adhesive applicator. Work in sections. Glue the tiles to the edge, applying them so the ridges on the back of each tile lie horizontal (perpendicular to the glue strokes) to help the tile hold its grip. The beveled edge of each tile should rise a bit above the edge of the tabletop.

Alternate the Pansy, Indigo, Dew and Glacier tiles in a random pattern, spacing them about ⅛" (3mm) apart. If the tiles keep falling off, you are using too much glue. Work quickly. Adjust the space between the tiles so that eighteen tiles fit along each edge. Let the adhesive dry.

12 FILL IN THE DESIGN

Glue border tiles on the top next, coordinating with the spacing of the side edge tiles. Then glue the decoratively shaped tiles over the rest of the surface, working in small sections and following the pattern. Keep the spaces between the tiles small.

You may need to trim tiles as you go to make them fit, especially the background tiles you use to fill small spaces. Use wooden craft sticks to apply adhesive in tight areas and to move the tiles into place on the pattern. Let the adhesive dry completely before proceeding.

13 APPLY THE GROUT

Follow the package's instructions to mix a full bag of grout. It should be the consistency of very thick cream. Apply the grout using a grout applicator spatula, making sure all the gaps are filled. Smooth the grout along the table edge with your fingers to give it an even, finished look. Let the grout set and dry for approximately twenty minutes.

14 REMOVE EXCESS GROUT

Clean the surface with the rubber edge of a mosaic sponge/float. Frequently rinse the sponge in a large bucket of clean water. When you are finished, dump the water outside; do not pour it down a drain.

15 CLEAN THE MOSAIC

Let the table dry and wipe the surface with a damp sponge to remove any film left by the grout. Repeat this step until you're satisfied. Rub a bit of olive oil on the mosaic once it is dry to add extra sheen to the glass tiles.

The Finished Tabletop

BOLT THE MOSAIC ONTO A TABLE BASE FOR A SPECTACULAR COURTYARD TABLETOP. DO NOT LET WATER SIT ON THE TABLE FOR EXTENDED PERIODS OF TIME, AND COVER IT OR BRING IT INDOORS DURING COLD WINTERS.

FRENCH BOTANICALS

THE FRENCH BOTANICAL GARDEN HAS A FUN, ALMOST WHIMSICAL AMBIANCE. AN OLD BIKE LEANING AGAINST A WALL WITH RED GERANIUMS GROWING FROM THE WICKER BASKET WOULD FIT RIGHT INTO THIS GARDEN. THE FLOWERS HERE MIGHT INCLUDE LILACS, MARIGOLDS, MINIATURE PINK ROSES, IRISES AND AN IVY TOPIARY IN THE SHAPE OF A HEART.

THE COLOR COMBINATIONS ARE INFLUENCED BY THE FRENCH COUNTRYSIDE. THEY INCLUDE CREAM, LAVENDER, PURPLE, SAGE GREEN, LEAF GREEN AND BRIGHT METALLIC COPPER ACCENTS. OLD BOTANICAL PRINTS, ENDLESS FIELDS OF FRAGRANT LAVENDER AND THE FLEUR-DE-LIS ARE ALL ICONS RELATED TO THIS STYLISH BUT CASUAL THEME.

LIKE THE OTHER PROJECTS IN THIS BOOK, THESE PLAY A PRACTICAL ROLE, ADDING BOTH BEAUTY AND FUNCTION TO YOUR DÉCOR. PRESERVE YOUR FLOWERS AND HERBS WITH A BEAUTIFUL DÉCOUPAGED FLOWER PRESS OR HANG THEM ON A PAINTED LAVENDER DRYING RACK. SERVE YOUR GUESTS FROM A BOTANICAL PRINT FERN TRAY OR CHECK THE WEATHER ON AN OUTDOOR THERMOMETER PLAQUE MADE WITH FRESHLY PRESSED ROSEMARY. THEN BRIGHTEN YOUR PATIO AND GARDEN WITH GLEAMING COPPER GARDEN STAKES AND TIN PLANTERS PAINTED WITH LAVENDER FIELDS.

LEONARDO DA VINCI AND BENJAMIN FRANKLIN BOTH WERE KNOWN TO MAKE BOTANICAL PRINTS USING THE SAME TECHNIQUE USED ON THIS COPPER-TRIMMED SERVING TRAY, A SIMPLE PROJECT FOR BEGINNERS AND NON-PAINTERS. ACCENT YOUR TRAY WITH INSECTS AND A LABEL PAINTED WITH THE BOTANICAL NAME OF THE PLANT. THEN COVER FERN LEAVES WITH PAINT TO PRINT ONTO THE TRAY. CHOOSE LEAVES THAT ARE RELATIVELY FLAT AND HAVE PROMINENT VEINS. PRESS THEM IN A HEAVY BOOK OVERNIGHT TO MAKE THEM EASIER TO HANDLE. SILK LEAVES ALSO YIELD GREAT RESULTS.

Botanical PRINT TRAY

BEFORE YOU BEGIN

❋ **Copper foil tape** *is available at craft and stained glass supply stores. The large rolls come in a variety of widths and have adhesive backing for easy application.*

❋ *A* **splatter brush** *is a specialty brush that creates fine splatters of paint across your surface. The soft, speckled effect enhances the overall design. You can substitute an ordinary toothbrush if you prefer. Thin the paint with water before loading the brush and practice on scrap paper until you are pleased with the effect.*

YOU WILL NEED

- ◆ 9" x 18" (23cm x 46cm) oval wooden tray

- ◆ brushes: 1" (25mm) flat for basecoating, no. 3 round

- ◆ acrylic paint (DecoArt Americana): Buttermilk, Hauser Medium Green, Celery Green, Reindeer Moss Green, Black Green, Metallic Copper, Titanium (Snow) White

- ◆ natural sea sponge

- ◆ wax paper

- ◆ fresh (or silk) ferns

- ◆ dense foam sponges (makeup sponges)

- ◆ low-tack masking tape

- ◆ insect patterns (page 116)

- ◆ transfer paper

- ◆ tracing stylus

- ◆ matte acrylic varnish

- ◆ permanent black pen

- ◆ splatter brush or an old toothbrush

- ◆ ½" and ³⁄₁₆" (13mm and 5mm) wide copper foil tape

1 PAINT THE TRAY
Basecoat the tray with Buttermilk paint and a basecoating brush. Mix Hauser Medium Green and Buttermilk on the palette with a sea sponge and tap it on the rim of the tray. Vary the shading, going from darker green at the top of the rim to lighter down by the base. Use the basecoating brush to work the paint into the seams if necessary.

2 SOFTEN THE EDGES
Sponge over the base of the tray with Buttermilk to soften the sponged edge. Let the tray dry completely.

3 SPONGE PAINT ONTO THE FERN
Put Hauser Medium Green, Celery Green and Reindeer Moss Green on your palette. Place a large fern frond on a sheet of scrap or wax paper. Apply various shades of green paint heavily onto the back of the fern with a dense foam sponge. If you have never made a leaf print before, practice on scrap paper first. Experiment with the amount of paint you use and the arrangement of the leaves until you are happy with the results.

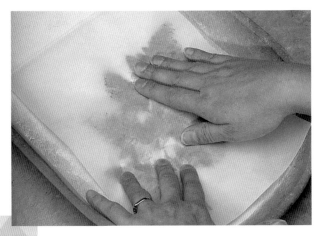

4 MAKE A FERN PRINT

Place the fern, paint side down, on the tray and cover it with a protective sheet of wax paper. Firmly press the painted leaf to make the print and let the tray dry.

5 TOUCH UP THE DESIGN

Carefully lift the wax paper and the fern. If the print is not perfect, use the same palette of greens and a no. 3 round brush to paint details—stems and leaf tips—that didn't transfer. Natural foliage imprints usually need less touching up than silk greenery imprints. Let the tray dry completely.

6 PAINT THE PLANT LABEL

At the base of the imprint, mask off a ¾" x 2½" (2cm x 6cm) rectangle with masking tape. Paint the space with Titanium (Snow) White to create a label. Remove the tape and let the paint dry.

7 PAINT THE INSECTS

Transfer the insect patterns to the tray with transfer paper and a tracing stylus. Paint them with Hauser Medium Green, Black Green and Metallic Copper paints and a no. 3 round brush. Let the paint dry completely.

8 VARNISH THE TRAY

Varnish the entire surface of the tray with matte varnish and a basecoating brush to protect your painting. If you make a mistake later when you add the splattering and lettering, varnishing the tray now will allow you to correct the mistake without damaging the work you've already done.

9 INSCRIBE THE LABEL

Hand letter the plant label with the botanical name for the plant using a permanent black pen. This is a bracken fern, or Pteridium aquilinum. Field guides and plant catalogs list the botanical names of common plants.

10 ANTIQUE WITH SPLATTERED COPPER

Thin some Metallic Copper paint with water and then splatter it onto the tray with a splatter brush or toothbrush.

11 TRIM THE SIDES WITH COPPER TAPE

Cut several pieces of ½" (13mm) copper foil tape. Each piece should be long enough to wrap from the base over the sides plus a ½" (13mm) of overlap to tuck under the tray. For tray sides that are 2" (5cm) tall, cut 5" (13cm) strips.

Remove the backing from the copper tape. Apply each strip starting from the inside base of the tray and smooth it into place. Space the strips about ½" (13mm) apart. When you get to the last 6 to 8" (15 to 20cm) of tray, start to eyeball the spacing between the strips to make sure they look even. You'll need about forty strips to complete a 9" x 18" (23cm x 46cm) tray.

LIVE PLANT VARIATION

Delicate impressions of fresh herbs create a very different effect on this variation. Notice that you can modify the copper tape embellishment for any size or style of tray.

12 FINISH THE EDGE

Trim the inside seam between the base and the sides of the tray with a strip of ³⁄₁₆" (5mm) copper tape. Remember to protect your tray from wear by coating it with several layers of good varnish.

The Finished Tray

YOUR TRAY IS CERTAIN TO BE ADMIRED AT YOUR NEXT SUMMER OUTDOOR GATHERING. IF YOU NEED TO CLEAN UP DIRT OR SPILLS, DO NOT IMMERSE THE TRAY IN WATER. SIMPLY WIPE IT CLEAN WITH A DAMP CLOTH.

Every home needs an outside thermometer, but so many are plain and utilitarian. This project offers a charming remedy: Mount the thermometer on an imitation slate plaque adorned with herbs and a winged insect. Simply imprint herbs, flowers and an insect charm into polymer clay. Bake and basecoat the clay with weatherproof acrylic paint and paint the herb, flower and insect shapes with sage, lavender and green paint.

Herb GARDEN THERMOMETER

BEFORE YOU BEGIN

❧ *This project uses* **weatherproof acrylic paints** *specially formulated for outdoor use. I used Patio Paint.*

❧ *A* **polymer clay roller** *is a smooth, hard roller made of wood or clear acrylic. Acrylic rollers are better because clay doesn't stick as much. Rubber rollers generally are too soft to work well with polymer clay.*

❧ *To create a thin wash, dilute your paint with the* **clear acrylic medium** *formulated for the line of paint you're using.*

YOU WILL NEED

- inexpensive outdoor thermometer that will come out of its base easily
- white polymer clay
- 10" (25cm) glazed tile as a work surface
- polymer clay roller
- fresh herb sprigs (fresh lavender, rosemary, sage and thyme are all good choices.)
- tiny silk flower blossoms
- brass insect charm
- rough-edged stone for texturing clay
- brushes: no. 4 round, no. 6 flat, ½" (13mm) flat
- weatherproof acrylic paints (DecoArt Patio Paint): Daisy Cream, Petunia Purple, Light Waterfall Blue, Light Sage Green, Fern Green and Old Brick Red
- clear acrylic medium
- paper towel
- thick scrap of wood
- drill with a ³⁄₁₆" (5mm) bit
- 14" (36cm) green garden twine
- silicone-based glue

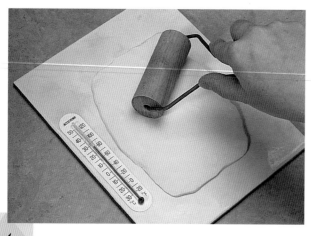

1 ROLL OUT THE CLAY

Condition the polymer clay following the instructions on page 12. Roll out the clay on a glazed ceramic tile with a polymer clay roller until you have a ¼" (6mm) thick sheet measuring roughly 4½" x 6½" (11cm x 17cm).

Carefully remove the thermometer from its base. Press it into the soft clay to mark its position and remove. Position it off center to leave room on one side to decorate.

2 PRESS HERBS INTO THE CLAY

Arrange some fresh herb sprigs, silk flowers and an insect charm on the clay next to the thermometer imprint. Roll over the items lightly with the roller to impress their images into the clay. You may need to push the charm in with your fingers to get a good impression. Carefully remove the herbs, flowers and charm.

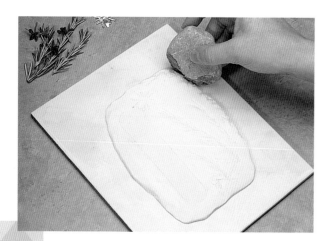

3 TEXTURE THE EDGES

Use a rock with a jagged edge to imprint a textured border on the edges of the clay so it looks like slate. Bake the clay following the instructions on page 13, leaving it on the tile for baking so it doesn't warp. Let the plaque cool.

4 PAINT THE PLAQUE

Basecoat the plaque with Daisy Cream paint and a ½" (13mm) flat brush. Paint over the plant details with no. 4 round and no. 6 flat brushes. Use Petunia Purple for the blossoms, Light Sage Green and Fern Green for the leaves and Light Waterfall Blue with a touch of Petunia Purple for the insect. Thin the paints with clear acrylic medium so it flows easily into the details. Wipe away unwanted paint with a damp towel.

5 ANTIQUE THE SURFACE

After the paint has dried completely, coat the entire surface with a a mixture of clear acrylic medium and a touch of Old Brick Red to antique the surface and accent the details.

6 DRILL HOLES TO HANG

Place the finished plaque on a thick scrap of wood and drill two 3/16" (5mm) holes at the top for the twine.

The Finished Plaque

THREAD THE GARDEN TWINE THROUGH THE HOLES AND TIE THE ENDS IN THE BACK. GLUE THE THERMOMETER ON WITH SILICONE-BASED GLUE SUITABLE FOR OUTDOOR USE. HANG YOUR FINISHED PLAQUE IN AN AREA WHERE YOU CAN EASILY READ THE THERMOMETER. THESE GARDEN PLAQUES MAKE PERFECT GIFTS FOR ANY OCCASION. YOU CAN MOUNT A BAROMETER INSTEAD, OR FEATURE A FAVORITE GARDEN PROVERB BY IMPRINTING RUBBER STAMP ALPHABETS INTO THE CLAY.

Transform galvanized tin vases with scenes of a charming French countryside that blooms with fields of fragrant lavender. The painting style is loose and suitable for beginners. This project is demonstrated on a slender, four-sided vase, but you can enlarge the pattern if you want to work on larger or different shaped containers. Copper tape not only makes a beautiful border accent, but also prevents slugs and snails from crawling in and eating your plants.

Lavender FIELDS VASE

BEFORE YOU BEGIN

❧ *This project uses* **acrylic paints for metal.** *Unlike ordinary acrylic paints, these need no primer or varnish and won't peel from metal. I used No-Prep Metal Paint.*

❧ *If you need to thin the paint, do not use water, as it weakens the paint. Instead, use the* **clear acrylic medium** *sold with metal paint.*

❧ *Metal paint has a tendency to dry a few shades darker than it first appears, so let it dry before moving on to the next step.*

❧ *A* **deer foot stippler** *is a brush with bristles cut to look like a deer's foot. Use a light, pouncing motion as you stipple so the bristles splay out, giving a very airy effect for shrubbery and soft, textured paint effects.*

❧ **Copper foil tape** *is available at craft and stained glass supply stores.*

YOU WILL NEED

◆ 8" (20cm) tall galvanized tin vase

◆ four square paint applicator sponges

◆ acrylic paints for metal (DecoArt No-Prep Metal Paint): Antique Lace, Ivory, Soft Blue, Heritage Blue, Fresh Lavender, Sage Green, Hunter Green, Artichoke Green, Burnt Sienna, Espresso Bean

◆ lavender fields pattern (page 118)

◆ tracing paper

◆ transfer paper

◆ tracing stylus

◆ masking tape

◆ brushes: no. 2 flat, ½" (13mm) flat, ¼" (6mm) deer foot stippler, ⅜" (10mm) deer foot stippler, various round brushes

◆ ³⁄₁₆" (5mm) copper foil tape (use wider tape for larger containers)

◆ clear acrylic medium (optional)

1 BASECOAT THE TIN VASE

Hold the vase with your hand inside so you don't smudge the paint. Apply Antique Lace metal paint along the top (near the opening) of the vase in a 3" (8cm) band using a small square sponge. While the paint is still wet, switch sponges and apply a band of Soft Blue below the Antique Lace. Softly blend the colors where they meet. Then sponge on a bottom band of a mixture of Heritage Blue and Fresh Lavender. Let the vase dry.

2 TRANSFER THE PATTERN

Copy the patterns onto tracing paper. Tape the pattern panels onto the sides of the vase in sequence. You'll have to use the patterns twice, so make sure you remember which pattern was used on which side of the vase. It helps to put tape on the bottom of the vase and number the sides and patterns. Place transfer paper under each pattern and trace only the two main landscape lines with a tracing stylus.

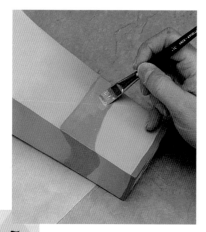

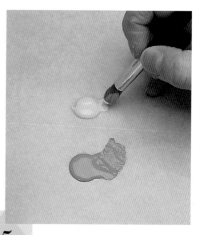

3 PAINT THE LANDSCAPE

Using a ½" (13mm) flat brush, paint the fields at the bottom of the vase with Sage Green. Paint the distant hills with a 50/50 mix of Fresh Lavender and Sage Green. Let the vase dry completely.

4 TRACE THE DETAILS

Place the transfer paper and tracing paper patterns back on the appropriate sides of the vase. Line up the patterns on the landscape lines. Trace the houses, trees and bushes with a tracing stylus.

5 LOAD THE STIPPLER

Pour separate puddles of Heritage Blue and Ivory paint onto your palette. Load a ⅜" (10mm) deer foot stippler with Heritage Blue, working the paint up into the bristles. Then dab the tip of the loaded brush into the Ivory paint.

6 ADD THE CLOUDS

With a pouncing motion, push the brush onto the vase to add the clouds. The paint will mix as you apply it, creating blue clouds tipped with a lighter ivory. Don't work the brush too much or the colors will mix together and you'll lose the effect. This paint technique is meant to be fun and loose. Don't worry about being perfect.

7 PAINT THE BUSHES AND HOUSES

Clean the brush, load it with Sage Green and tip it with Antique Lace to paint the green bushes. Paint the sunny sides of the houses with a no. 2 flat brush and Ivory and the shady sides with a no. 2 flat brush and a mixture of Ivory and Heritage Blue. Paint the roofs Burnt Sienna. Load a ⅜" (10mm) deer foot stippler brush with Sage Green and tip it with Fresh Lavender. Stipple the rows of lavender bushes in the fields.

8 ADD THE DETAILS

Add the windows with the no. 2 flat brush and Espresso Bean paint. Paint the cypress trees with a ¼" (6mm) deer foot stippler, picking up Hunter Green and Artichoke Green alternately to create variety. Work upside down on the vase and start at the base of each tree. Then touch up any spots necessary with round brushes and let the vase dry completely.

The Finished Vase

TRIM THE TOP AND BOTTOM EDGES OF THE VASE WITH ³⁄₁₆" (5MM) WIDE COPPER FOIL TAPE.

A PLANT PRESS CAN BE A DECORATIVE ACCENT AS WELL AS A PRACTICAL TOOL. OR USE IT AS A WELCOME GIFT FOR A FELLOW GARDENER OR AN EDUCATIONAL PROJECT FOR SOMEONE LEARNING TO PRESS PLANTS. SPEND THE EXTRA TIME TO DÉCOUPAGE A PLANT PRESS WITH PRESSED FLOWERS, BOTANICAL TRANSFERS AND HANDMADE PAPERS SO YOU CAN DISPLAY IT PROUDLY AS AN ATTRACTIVE ACCENT.

Découpaged FLOWER PRESS

BEFORE YOU BEGIN

❧ **White Lightning** *is a sealer and white stain in one. It creates a semitransparent, whitewashed effect. You can purchase White Lightning in craft stores.*

❧ *Use a* **smooth, absorbent paper***, such as rice paper, inside your flower press. The texture from paper towels will imprint itself onto the pressed flowers and leaves. Smooth papers are available in rolls or sheets at fine art stores.*

❧ *Pressing your own flowers to decorate the press is best, but you can also find* **pressed flowers** *at craft stores in the floral department.*

❧ **Lazertran** *is a transfer paper that creates detailed color image transfers on a variety of craft surfaces. Copy any image onto Lazertran paper using a photocopier (not an inkjet printer) and soak it in water to create a water-slide decal. Lazertran is available at craft stores.*

YOU WILL NEED

- ◆ two 12" x 9" (30cm x 23cm) matching wooden plaques
- ◆ brushes: no. 4 round, 1" (25mm) foam brush, 1" (25mm) flat for basecoating
- ◆ White Lightning varnish
- ◆ medium (100-grit) sandpaper
- ◆ large, heavy-duty rubber bands
- ◆ thick scrap of wood
- ◆ drill with ¼" (6mm) and ⅜" (10mm) drill bits
- ◆ four 3" x ³⁄₁₆" (8cm x 5mm) machine screws, four matching washers and four wing nuts
- ◆ strong wood glue
- ◆ four 1" (3cm) flat top wooden knobs
- ◆ sheet of green handmade paper
- ◆ sheet of natural, or tan, handmade paper
- ◆ thin-bodied white glue
- ◆ assorted botanical clip art images (see pages 124-125)
- ◆ Lazertran image transfer paper
- ◆ scissors
- ◆ bowl of clean, warm water
- ◆ paper towels
- ◆ sheet of cream card stock
- ◆ small pressed flowers: fern, primrose, larkspur, violet and lobelia
- ◆ black permanent pen
- ◆ clear acrylic varnish
- ◆ twenty sheets of 8½" x 11" (22cm x 28cm) smooth, absorbent paper
- ◆ ten sheets of 8½" x 11" (22cm x 28cm) thin corrugated cardboard

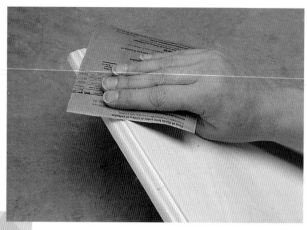

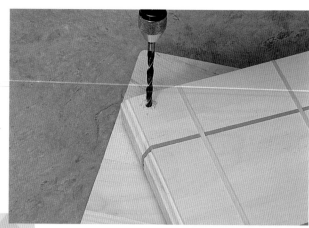

1 BASECOAT THE BOARDS

Paint the tops and sides of the two plaques with White Lightning varnish and a basecoating brush. The tinted varnish will whiten but not completely cover the grain of the natural wood. Do not paint the bottoms of the plaques. The unpainted surfaces achieve better airflow for using the press to dry flowers. Let the boards dry completely, then sand the edges to distress them and reveal some of the natural wood color.

2 DRILL THE CORNER HOLES

Wrap the boards together with rubber bands and mark each corner 1" (3cm) in from the corner edge. Place the boards on a thick scrap of wood and drill ¼" (6mm) wide holes through both boards at each corner.

Countersink the holes with the ⅜" (10mm) drill bit so the wooden knobs will sit flush with the surface. Remove the rubber bands and mark the insides of the boards so you'll always know which ends go together.

3 GLUE ON THE WOODEN FEET

Elevate the bottom plaque, drop a machine screw into each hole and glue them into place. Then apply a strong wood glue to the bolt heads and secure the wooden knobs over the bolts. Let the glue dry completely.

4 TEAR THE HANDMADE PAPER

Tear the green handmade paper into five panels approximately 2½" (6cm) square. To tear the handmade paper, dip a round brush into clean water and brush lines along the paper. Tear the paper along the wet lines to easily create panels with a natural edge. Tear the tan handmade paper into five panels measuring about 3" x 2¼" (8cm x 6cm).

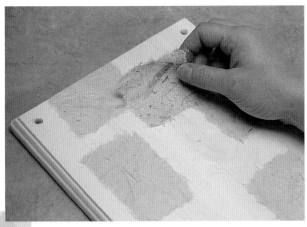

5 GLUE THE PANELS ONTO THE PLAQUE
Using the white glue and foam brush, glue the handmade panels onto the top plaque. Start with the tan panels and overlap the green panels in a random pattern.

6 WET THE BOTANICAL IMAGE TRANSFERS
Photocopy a page of botanical clip art images onto Lazertran transfer paper using brown toner. Follow the manufacturer's directions to ensure you copy the image onto the correct side of the transfer paper. Cut out five individual botanical motifs and drop them into a bowl of warm water.

7 APPLY THE IMAGE TRANSFERS
Remove the Lazertran paper from the water after 20 or 30 seconds or once it starts to curl. Slide the images off their paper backing onto the plaque top, layering them over the handmade papers in a pleasing arrangement. Use a paper towel to gently remove excess water and let dry.

8 ADD THE PRESSED FLOWERS
Cut the cream card stock into five panels of varying sizes and shapes. Glue them among the transfer images on the plaque top. Using a foam brush, paint a very thin coat of white glue over each cream panel. Let the glue tack up a bit and then carefully place pressed flowers on the panels. Use very little glue or the excess moisture will discolor and wrinkle the pressed flowers.

9 COAT THE FLOWERS WITH GLUE
Gently cover the flowers with a very light coating of glue to protect them from the excess moisture of the varnish. Let the glue dry.

10 EMBELLISH THE BORDERS
Add lines around the card stock flower panels with a black permanent pen to dress them up. Varnish the entire top of the plaque to protect the collage, following the instructions on page 18.

The Finished Flower Press

PLACE TWO SHEETS OF SMOOTH, ABSORBENT PAPER BETWEEN TWO PIECES OF THIN CARDBOARD. CONTINUE THIS PATTERN UNTIL YOU'VE USED TWENTY PIECES OF PAPER AND TEN PIECES OF CARDBOARD. TRIM THE CORNERS SO THE STACK FITS INTO THE PRESS. PLACE THE TOP PLAQUE IN POSITION OVER THE STACK OF PAPER AND CARDBOARD AND SECURE IT WITH THE WASHERS AND WING NUTS.

HOW TO PRESS PLANTS & FLOWERS

Pressing plants is a simple drying method that results in two-dimensional blossoms and leaves for mounting on cards and labels or displaying under glass. Harvest the plants in the morning after the morning dew has dried. Collect flowers, as well as the leaves and buds of the plant, in various stages of bloom. Thinner flowers work best. Press the plants as soon as possible after harvesting to prevent wilting. Different flowers take a variety of different times to dry, which can range from two to three weeks.

1 PLACE FLOWERS IN THE PRESS

Place fresh flowers into the press between the sheets of smooth, absorbent paper. Sandwich these sheets between the cardboard sheets. Keep filling and stacking the flowers, papers and cardboard until the press is full. Press the top plaque down onto the pages and tighten the wing nuts.

2 PERIODICALLY TIGHTEN THE PRESS

After two days, push the top plaque down and tighten the wing nuts again. Do this every few days until the moisture has been squeezed out and you cannot push the press down any further. You'll need to do this one to three times depending on the flowers you're pressing. Flowers that are firmly pressed as they dry will have the best color retention and smooth, flat petals.

3 REMOVE THE FLOWERS WHEN DRY

Check the press in about two weeks. You won't harm the process if you leave the plants in the press after they have dried, but you can damage them if the drying process has not been completed. After the flowers have dried completely, remove the pressed flowers with tweezers and store flat in labeled envelopes.

RECOMMENDED PLANTS FOR PRESSING

• Columbine	• Fern, all types	• Leaves, all types	• Sage flowers
• Coralbell	• Forget-Me-Not	• Lily of the Valley	• Statice
• Cosmos	• Freesia	• Lobelia	• Sweet Alyssum
• Daisy	• Geranium	• Pansy	• Sweet Pea
• Delphinium	• Hydrangea blossoms	• Primrose	• Violet
• Dusty Miller	• Larkspur	• Queen Anne's Lace	• Wild Rose

ENJOY THE BEAUTY AND SWEET SCENT OF HERBS YEAR ROUND.

DECORATE THIS PLAQUE WITH A PAINTED BUNDLE OF LAVENDER AND

FLEUR-DE-LIS HOOKS FOR DRYING HERBS AND FLOWERS. THE EASY, LOOSE

PAINTING TECHNIQUE IS FUN AND EASY FOR BEGINNING PAINTERS. YOU'LL LAY

DOWN A SERIES OF LIGHT WASHES THAT BECOME DARKER AND MORE OPAQUE

AS YOU ADD THE FINISHING BRUSHSTROKES, ALLOWING YOU TO GENTLY BUILD

UP THE PAINTING.

Lavender DRYING RACK

BEFORE YOU BEGIN

✤ **Copper wire** *is available at craft stores in different thicknesses, or gauges. The higher the gauge, the thinner the wire.*

✤ **Blue water-erasable transfer paper** *allows you to erase pattern lines once you're done with them. You also can use regular transfer paper.*

YOU WILL NEED

- ◆ 12" x 20" (30cm x 51cm) French Provincial wooden sign board

- ◆ brushes: no. 1, no. 4 and no. 6 rounds, no. 4 flat, 1" (25mm) flat for basecoating

- ◆ acrylic paint (DecoArt Americana): Shale Green, Jade Green, Blue Haze, Lavender, Violet Haze, Sapphire, Royal Purple, Burnt Sienna, Hauser Medium Green, Arbor Green, Plantation Pine, Baby Blue

- ◆ masking tape

- ◆ freezer paper

- ◆ paint spatula

- ◆ 4" (10cm) dense foam roller

- ◆ lavender pattern (page 121)

- ◆ tracing paper

- ◆ transfer paper

- ◆ tracing stylus

- ◆ three 1½" (4cm) embossed wooden fleur-de-lis

- ◆ double-sided tape

- ◆ medium (100-grit) sandpaper

- ◆ 18- and 22-gauge copper wire

- ◆ wire cutters

- ◆ white craft glue

- ◆ clear acrylic varnish

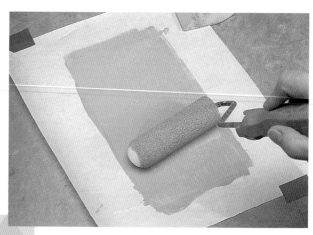

1 BASECOAT THE PLAQUE

Follow the instructions on pages 8 and 9 to seal the wood plaque and apply two basecoats of Shale Green with a basecoating brush. Let the plaque dry before proceeding.

2 LOAD THE ROLLER WITH PAINT

Tape freezer paper to your work surface. Pour puddles of Shale Green and Jade Green next to each other at the top of the freezer paper. Use a paint spatula to pull the paint down in parallel bands. Using a dense foam roller, blend the paint until the roller is loaded and the paint mixed together in the middle. You're going after a graded effect, not two separate lines of color.

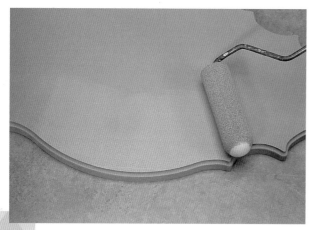

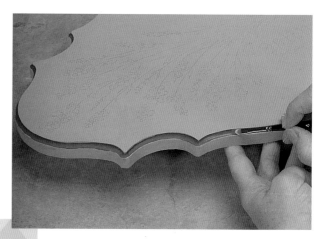

3 APPLY THE JADE GREEN BORDER

Roll the paint around the border of the plaque with the Shale Green on the inside and the Jade Green at the edge. This is a very easy way to get a beautiful blended effect around the border of the plaque. Let the paint dry completely.

4 PAINT THE TRIM

Copy the lavender pattern and follow the instructions on page 10 to transfer it to the plaque. Paint Blue Haze on the trim with a no. 4 flat brush.

5 PAINT THE STEMS AND FLOWERS

Paint the flower heads with a no. 6 round brush and a light wash of Lavender thinned with a bit of water. With the same brush, paint in the stems with a wash of Burnt Sienna.

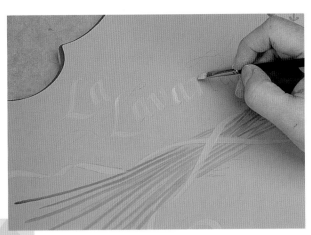

6 PAINT THE RIBBONS AND LETTERS

Load a no. 4 flat brush with Baby Blue paint; don't thin it. Use the chisel edge—the long, flat edge—of the brush to paint the ribbons and letters.

7 ADD THE LEAVES AND BLOSSOM HIGHLIGHTS

Paint the leaves with a wash of Hauser Medium Green and the no. 4 round brush. Then add highlights to the tips of the lavender blossoms using the no. 4 round brush and a wash of Violet Haze.

8 COLOR THE BLOSSOM CENTERS

Mix Sapphire and Violet Haze and dab the lavender blossom centers on the flowers with a no. 4 round brush.

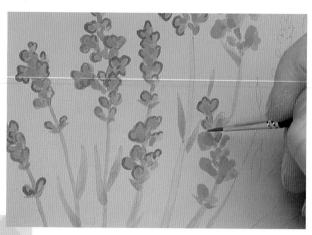

9 ADD TINY LEAVES
Load the no. 4 round with Hauser Medium Green, and add tiny leaves to the base of each blossom to attach the blossoms to the stems.

10 FINISH THE BLOSSOMS
Load a no. 1 round brush with Royal Purple and outline the lavender blossom edges to emphasize and add contrast to the flowers.

11 SHADE AND HIGHLIGHT THE LEAVES
Shade one side of each leaf with a wash of Plantation Pine and the no. 4 round brush. Then add some highlights to the leaves with Arbor Green.

12 SHADE AND HIGHLIGHT THE RIBBONS
Use a no. 4 flat brush and a wash of Blue Haze to add depth to the ribbon. Make the underlying ribbon piece darker to contrast the top ribbon. Add lighter highlights to the ribbon with Baby Blue.

13 EMBELLISH THE LETTERS

Outline the letters with a no. 1 round and Blue Haze. If the letters appear too bright, add washes of Blue Haze with a no. 4 flat brush to tone them down.

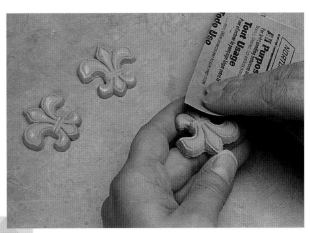

14 PAINT AND SAND THE HOOK BASES

Paint three wooden fleur-de-lis with Jade Green. Use double-sided tape to attach the wooden pieces to a piece of freezer paper to hold them still as you paint. When dry, sand the edges to give them a distressed look.

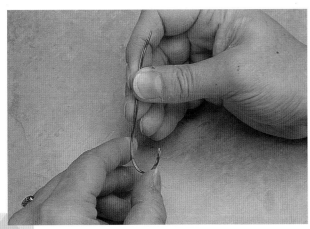

15 FORM THE HOOK

Fold a 10" (25cm) piece of 18-gauge copper wire in half and then bend the two strands to form a hook.

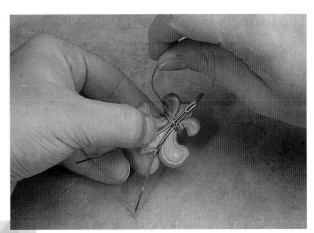

16 ATTACH THE HOOK TO THE HOOK BASE

Place the hook on top of the fleur-de-lis and wrap an 8" (20cm) piece of 22-gauge copper wire around them to hold them together.

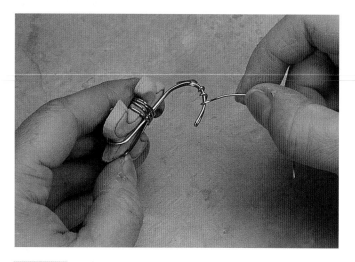

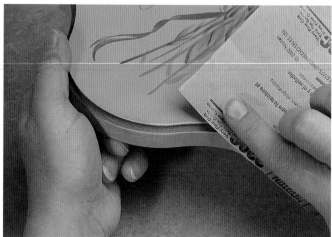

17 FINISH THE HOOKS

Tuck the loose ends of the hook behind each petal, so the sharp ends of the wire sit behind the fleur-de-lis. Strengthen the bent part of the hook by wrapping 22-gauge copper wire around it.

Repeat steps 15 through 17 to attach hooks to two more fleur-de-lis. Glue the three hooks to the rack in an attractive and functional arrangement below the design. Let the glue dry completely.

18 DISTRESS AND VARNISH THE PLAQUE

Sand the edges of the drying rack to give it a soft, weathered look. Varnish the plaque with two coats of clear acrylic varnish following the directions on page 18.

The Finished Drying Rack

YOUR RACK WILL LOOK BEAUTIFUL DISPLAYED IN THE KITCHEN WITH LARGE BUNDLES OF DRIED HERBS OR FLOWERS HANGING FROM ITS HOOKS. IF YOU PREFER TO HANG THE RACK OUTDOORS, PROTECT IT FROM THE ELEMENTS BY HANGING IT UNDER A PROTECTIVE AWNING, OUT OF DIRECT SUNLIGHT.

HOW TO DRY HERBS & FLOWERS

YOU CAN FIND DRIED HERBS AND FLOWERS IN STORES, BUT THEY WILL NEVER BE AS GOOD AS THE FRESHLY DRIED BOTANICALS YOU CREATE IN YOUR OWN HOME. WHEN YOU DRY YOUR OWN HERBS AND FLOWERS, THEY'LL HAVE BRIGHTER COLORS, THEY WON'T BE CRUSHED FROM TRANSPORTING AND THE AROMAS AND FLAVORS WILL BE MORE INTENSE.

AIR-DRYING PLANTS IS ONE OF THE EASIEST METHODS OF PRESERVING LEAVES AND BLOSSOMS. FOR THE BEST RESULTS, HARVEST FLOWERS JUST BEFORE FULL BLOOM. CUT THEM IN THE MORNING WHEN THE DEW HAS DRIED AND THE FLOWERS HAVE OPENED. AVOID PLANTS THAT ARE PAST THEIR PRIME OR HAVE INSECT OR DISEASE DAMAGE.

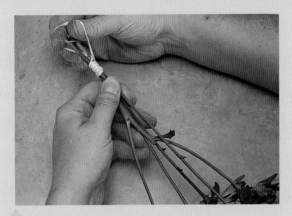

1 STRIP THE LEAVES OFF THE STEMS
Strip the leaves from the bottom of the stems where the bunch will be bound. This increases the strength of the stems and speeds up the drying time. Many leaves on flower stems become too brittle when dried, so leave just a few on the stem.

2 BAND THE STEMS TOGETHER AND HANG
Gather a bunch of five to seven stems, making sure that the herb or flower heads have sufficient air circulation. Secure the stems with a rubber band 1" to 2" (3cm to 5cm) from the end. Hang your plants in a dark, dry room with good ventilation. The darkness helps prevent the colors from fading. Your flowers are dry when the stems snap easily. Most flowers take up to three weeks to dry completely.

RECOMMENDED PLANTS FOR DRYING

• Baby's Breath	• Dusty Miller	• Lavender	• Statice
• Carnation	• Foxglove	• Marigold	• Strawflower
• Celosia	• Globe Amaranth	• Nigella seed heads	• Tansy
• Chive blossoms	• Goldenrod	• Peony	• Thistle
• Cornflower	• Heather	• Poppy seed heads	• Yarrow
• Dahlia	• Hydrangea	• Pussy Willow	• Zinnia
• Delphinium	• Larkspur	• Rose	

THIS BRIGHT COPPER STAKE WITH A CLASSIC FLEUR-DE-LIS MOTIF CAN ACCENT YOUR GARDEN AND PROTECT YOUR PLANTS. PLANT PROTECTORS ARE PLACED AT THE CORNERS OF VEGETABLE OR FLOWERBEDS TO PREVENT A GARDEN HOSE FROM DRAGGING OVER THE PLANTS. PLACE THE COPPER TUBE BASE OVER A METAL STAKE SO THAT IT ROTATES FREELY AS THE HOSE DRAGS AGAINST IT. THE PROJECT USES COPPER PLUMBING TUBES AND WIRE THAT ARE READILY AVAILABLE AT YOUR LOCAL HARDWARE STORE. NO SOLDERING IS REQUIRED; INSTEAD AN EASY TO USE EPOXY PUTTY SECURES THE DECORATIVE TOP.

Copper GARDEN STAKE

BEFORE YOU BEGIN

❧ **Seven-strand copper cable** *is a high-speed telecommunication cable found at hardware stores and generally sold by the foot.*

❧ *Use* **pipe connectors** *to connect different sizes of pipes together. Choose a copper connector so that it matches the copper pipes. You can also find these in your local hardware store.*

❧ **Epoxy putty** *creates a strong, waterproof bond and is more durable than polymer clay for outside use. I used Kneadatite epoxy putty because it cures to be slightly flexible and does not snap under stress. You can find it at hardware stores in the plumbing department.*

YOU WILL NEED

◆ 60" (152cm) of seven-strand copper cable

◆ wire cutters

◆ needle-nose pliers

◆ fleur-de-lis pattern (page 121)

◆ 22-gauge copper wire

◆ hammer

◆ anvil or hard surface

◆ epoxy putty

◆ ½" (13mm) copper pipe connector

◆ 30" (76cm) copper pipe, ½" (13mm) in diameter

◆ petroleum jelly

◆ soft brush

◆ metallic powder (Pearl-Ex): Super Copper

1 CUT THE CABLES

Cut two 11" (28cm) sections of copper cable with a pair of wire cutters. Squeeze the wire cutters on the cable and bend the cable back and forth until metal fatigue breaks the wire cleanly.

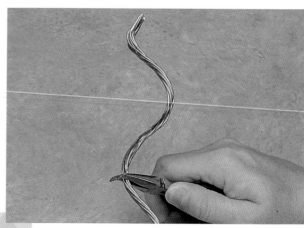

2 SHAPE THE CABLES

Follow the fleur-de-lis pattern and bend the two cable pieces into matching curves with needle-nose pliers.

3 JOIN THE TWO PIECES

Place these two curved pieces together and wrap a piece of 22-gauge wire around the top and center six or seven times to join them. This will become the center of the fleur-de-lis motif.

4 TRIM THE WIRE ENDS

Twist the loose ends of the 22-gauge wire together and cut them short with wire cutters. When cutting wire, no matter what gauge, try to hold both ends to prevent a piece of wire from becoming airborne. Tuck in the end.

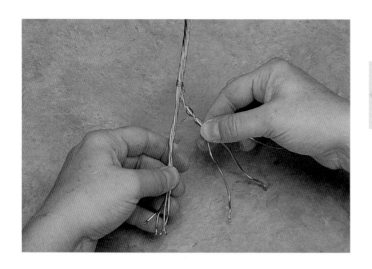

5 CUT AND JOIN TWO MORE CABLES
Cut two 12" (31cm) pieces of the copper cable for the sides of the fleur-de-lis motif. Wrap an 8" (20cm) length of 22-gauge wire around each cable several times, about four inches (10cm) up from the bottom of each piece. Separate the lower part of each cable into a four-strand piece and a three-strand piece.

6 DIVIDE THE TOP AND CURL THE SECTIONS
Divide the top part of the cable into three sections, one with three strands and two with two strands. Bend the two lower of these sections down into graceful curves and twist the ends together so that they form a curl. Check the pattern for size and shape.

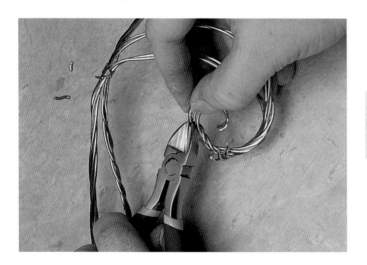

7 FINISH THE TOP CURL
Curve the top section down over the first two, wrapping the ends around the other sections to join them together. Trim any wire ends that stick out.

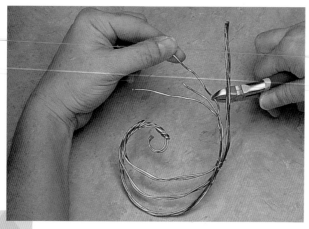

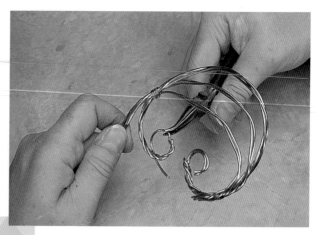

8 TRIM THE LOWER STRANDS
Turn the piece upside down. You still have the two sections you separated in step 5 to work with. Separate the three-strand section into individual strands and cut them to three different lengths: 3½", 2¾" and 2" (9cm, 7cm and 5cm).

9 FORM THE LOWER CURL
Twist these different sized strands together with pliers to create a smaller tapered curl. You still have a four-strand section to work with. Repeat steps 5 through 9 to shape the other 12" (30cm) cable.

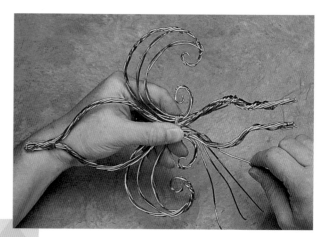

10 BIND THE PIECES
Place the finished side pieces on opposite sides of the center section and bind them together in the middle with a 10" (25cm) piece of 22-gauge wire.

11 WRAP THE LOOSE WIRES
Wrap the remaining eight loose strands of cable around the lower halves of the main section.

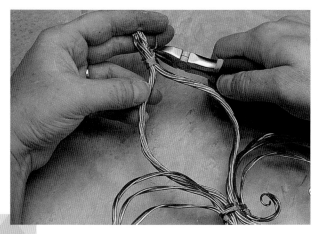

12 TAPER THE TOP

Snip a few strands from the top of the motif to thin it out.

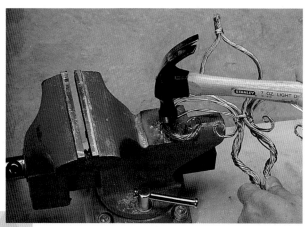

13 HAMMER THE MOTIF FLAT

Place the entire fleur-de-lis on an anvil or another smooth, hard surface and pound it flat with a hammer to stiffen, strengthen and hold the shape.

14 PREPARE THE EPOXY

Cut a 3" (8cm) section of two-part epoxy putty, remove the protective plastic and mix until the colors blend into a single color. You now have about one to two hours, at room temperature, to work with it before the epoxy cures to a hard consistency. You can prevent the epoxy putty from sticking to your fingers by applying petroleum jelly on your hands. Use it sparingly, though. The putty bonds well with contact to the wire as long as you don't use too much petroleum jelly.

15 MOUNT THE FLEUR-DE-LIS

Stuff the epoxy and the base of the fleur-de-lis into the wider end of a ½" (13mm) copper pipe connector.

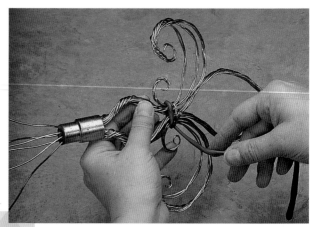

16 INSERT WIRES IN THE OPPOSITE END
Cut a 6" (15cm) section of cable. Unravel the seven strands and insert them into the epoxy putty in the other side of the pipe connector.

17 COIL PUTTY AROUND THE MOTIF
Cut another 3" (8cm) piece of epoxy putty tape. Mix and roll it into a thin, 12" (30cm) long strand. Wrap this strand around the center of the motif where the wire joins the pieces together.

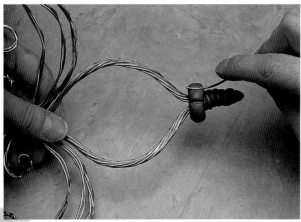

18 WRAP THE TOP WITH PUTTY
Cut a final 3" (8cm) piece of epoxy putty tape and mix the two parts together. Wrap the putty around the top of the fleur-de-lis to form a finial. Add decorative coils and press in details with a piece of wire.

19 BRUSH PUTTY WITH COPPER POWDER
Immediately, while the epoxy is still soft, brush all the exposed epoxy putty sections with copper metallic powder.

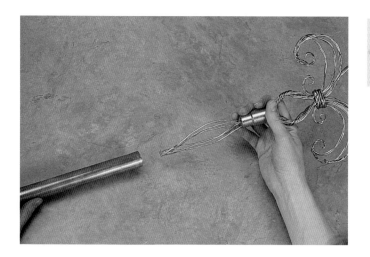

20 CONNECT THE TOP TO THE BASE

Bind the ends of the wires that are in the base of the pipe connector with 22-gauge wire. Allow the wires to bow out slightly in the center. Insert the fleur-de-lis top into the copper pipe. The pressure of the bowed wires will hold the top in place.

Creating a Weathered Patina

Pure copper turns green with age, but many copper pipes and tubing are made with a mixture of metals, causing them to turn a dark color instead of green. To get the desired color, you can create your own patina. Test scrap pieces of pipe, cable and wire first by spraying them with a 50/50 mixture of white vinegar and ammonia. This mixture will give pure copper an aged green patina instantly.

If you like the results, spray the finished piece and let it dry before placing outdoors. You can also create a faux patina by sponging on several shades of green metal paint.

The Finished Garden Stake

MOUNT THE FINISHED STAKE IN YOUR GARDEN BY PLACING THE COPPER TUBE BASE OVER A METAL STAKE. OVER TIME, YOUR COPPER GARDEN STAKE WILL DEVELOP A BEAUTIFUL WEATHERED GREEN PATINA. MAKE TWO OR THREE MATCHING STAKES AND GROUP THEM TOGETHER FOR A MORE DRAMATIC LOOK.

PATTERNS

The following pages include all the patterns you will need to complete the projects in this book. Most of these patterns are reduced in size. The captions list the percentage enlargement for each pattern to make it the correct size for your project. For instructions on transferring patterns to a project surface or making a stencil from a pattern, see pages 10 and 11.

This pattern is for the Mosaic Garden Table project on page 72. Enlarge the pattern 200%, then enlarge again 125% before transferring it to your surface.

These insect patterns are for the Botanical Print Tray on page 80. Copy these patterns at 154% before you transfer your pattern to the surface.

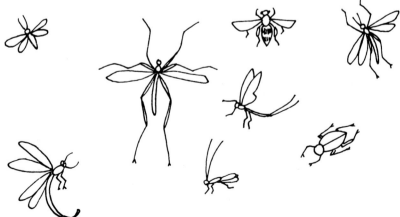

These patterns are for the pea pod on the Handmade Garden Journal on page 44. Transfer this pattern onto cardstock as they appear here and cut the pieces out to create your templates.

These patterns are for the Stenciled Pear Apron on page 22. Enlarge the patterns 200% before making your stencils.

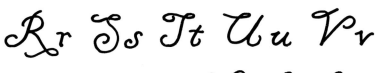

Aa Bb Cc Dd Ee Ff
Gg Hh Ii Jj Kk Ll
Mm Nn Oo Pp Qq
Rr Ss Tt Uu Vv

Forelle   Leckel

Chojure   Bartlett

Jargonelle   Doyenne

Angevine   Bosc

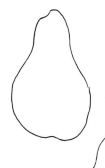

PEARS

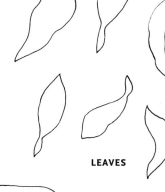

LEAVES

TWIGS AND BRANCH

This pattern is for the Lavender Fields Vase on page 90. Enlarge the pattern 182% before transferring it to your surface. To transfer the pattern onto a round vase instead of a square one, do not divide the pattern into four separate sections.

These phrases are for the Vegetable Patch Floor Cloth on page 38. Enlarge them 167% before transferring them to your surface.

Hoe, Hoe, Hoe.

Life is a Garden Welcome

These patterns are for the Vegetable Patch Floor Cloth on page 38. Enlarge them 200% before you transfer them to your surface.

CABBAGE

LADYBUGS

EGGPLANT

ONION

RADISHES

SPROUTS

CARROT

BEANS

PEAS

TOMATO

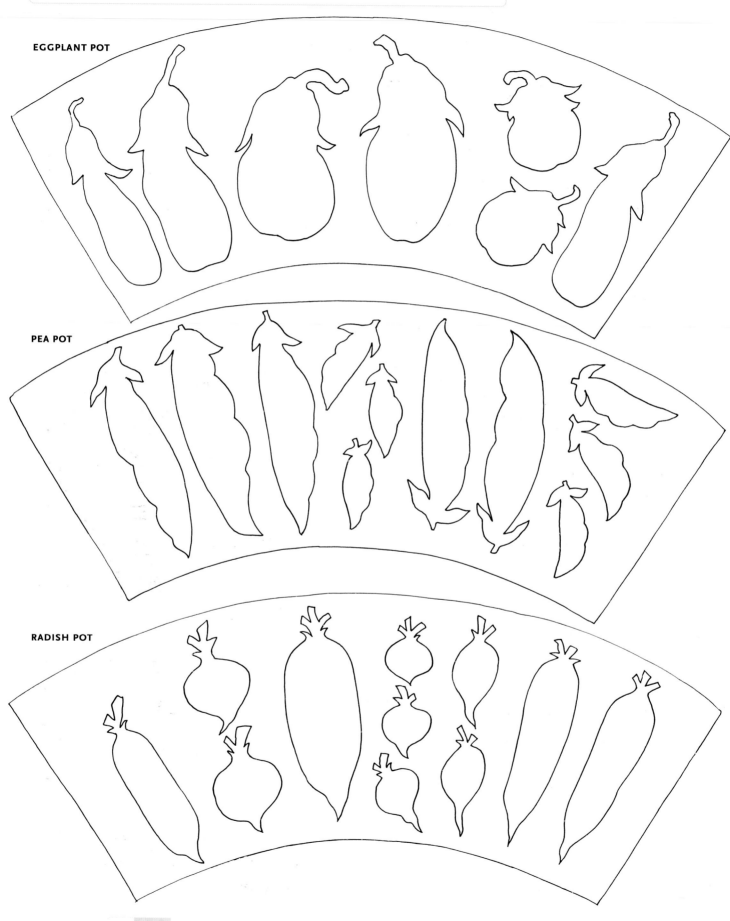

These patterns are for the Vegetable Etched Pots project on page 27.
Enlarge them 200% before transferring them to your surface.

EGGPLANT POT

PEA POT

RADISH POT

This pattern is for the Lavender Drying Rack on page 100. Enlarge it 174% before transferring it.

11" (28CM) CENTER PIECES (MAKE TWO)

12" (31CM) SIDE PIECES (MAKE TWO)

3 STRANDS

2 STRANDS

2 STRANDS

3 STRANDS

This pattern is for the Copper Garden Stake on page 108. It is full size. Use it as a guide to shape the copper cables.

These patterns are for the Sand Mosaic Tiles on page 68. Enlarge the patterns 200%. Enlarge the patterns again 125% before transferring them to your tiles.

FIG TILE PATTERN

LEMON TILE PATTERN

GRAPE TILE PATTERN

PEAR TILE PATTERN

123

RESOURCES

You will find a complete list of the supplies you need at the beginning of each project. Most are readily available at your local craft, fine art and home improvement stores. If you have difficulty locating the necessary supplies, look at this list of specialty suppliers and manufacturers for contact information so you can learn where they distribute their wares near you. Their Web sites also contain technical product support and other useful information.

BAGWORKS INC.
3301 S. Cravens Road, Bldg. C
Ft. Worth, TX 76119
Tel: 800 365-7423
Fax: 800 678-7364
www.bagworks.com
E-mail: info@bagworks.com
❧ *Gardener's muslin apron*
❧ *Floor cloths*

BOUTIQUE TRIMS, INC.
21200 Pontiac Trail
South Lyon, MI 48178
Tel: 248 437-2017
Fax: 248 437-9463
www.boutiquetrims.com
E-mail: info@btcrafts.com
❧ *Charms*

DecoArt
P.O. Box 386
Stanford, KY 40484
Tel: 606 365-3193
Fax: 606 365-9730
www.decoart.com
E-mail: paint@decoart.com
❧ *Patio Paint*
❧ *No-Prep Metal paint*
❧ *Americana acrylic paints*

DOVER PUBLICATIONS
31 E 2nd Street
Mineola, NY 11501
Tel: 516 294-7000
Fax: 516 742-5049
www.doverpublications.com
E-mail: fmure@doverpublications.com
❧ *Copyright-free botanical images from
Heck's Pictorial Archive of Nature and
Science and Plants and Flowers: 1,761
Illustrations for Artists and Designers*

DUNCAN ENTERPRISES
5673 E. Shields Avenue
Fresno, CA 93727
Tel: 559 291-4444
Fax: 559 291-9444
www.duncan-enterprises.com
❧ *General craft glue*

ENVIRONMENTAL TECHNOLOGIES
300 South Bay Depot Road
Fields Landing, CA 95537
Tel: 707 443-9323
Fax: 707 443-7962
www.eti-usa.com
E-mail: mail@eti-usa.com
❧ *Envirotex Lite (two-part resin)*
❧ *Ultra Seal (thin white glue)*
❧ *Rug Backing*

FISKARS BRANDS, INC.
7811 W. Stewart Avenue
Wausau, WI 54401
Tel: 715 842-2091
Fax: 715 848-5528
www.fiskars.com
❧ *Craft knives*
❧ *Decoupage scissors*
❧ *Rotary cutters*
❧ *Cutting mats*
❧ *Embossing stylus*

HERO ARTS
1343 Powell Street
Emeryville, CA 94608
Tel: 510 652-6055
Fax: 510 653-8620
www.heroarts.com
❧ *Castle Icons and Vintage Alphabet
rubber stamp sets*

HUNT CORP.
2005 Market Street
Philadelphia, PA 19103
Tel: 215 656-0300
Fax: 215 656-3700
www.hunt-corp.com
❧ *Paint pens*

JACQUARD PRODUCTS/
RUBERT GIBBON & SPIDER
P.O. Box 425
Healdsburg, CA 95448
Tel: 707 433-9577
Fax: 707 433-4906
www.jacquardproducts.com
❧ *Pearl-Ex powder*

KRYLON
101 Prospect Avenue, N.W.
Cleveland, OH 44115
Tel: 800 832-2541
Fax: 216 515-5545
www.krylon.com
❧ *Matte spray*

KUNIN FELT, FOSS
MANUFACTURING COMPANY, INC.
380 Lafayette Road
P.O. Box 5000
Hampton, NH 03843-5000
Tel: 603 929-6100
Fax: 603 929-6180
E-mail: Kuninfelt@fossmfg.com
❧ *Floor cloth material, roll or precut*

LAZERTRAN LLC
650 8th Avenue
New Hyde Park, NY 11040
Tel: 800 245-7547
Fax: 516 488-7898
www.lazertran.com
❧ *Transfer decal paper*

LEE VALLEY TOOLS
P.O. Box 1780
Ogdensburg, NY 13669-6780
US Tel: 800 267-8735
US Fax: 800 513-7885
CN Tel: 800 267-8761
CN Fax: 800 668-1807
www.leevalley.com
E-mail: customerservice@leevalley.com
❧ *Watchmaker's tins*
❧ *Metal card/label frame*

LOEW-CORNELL, INC.
563 Chestnut Avenue
Teaneck, NJ 07666
Tel: 201 836-7070
Fax: 201 836-8110
www.loew-cornell.com
E-mail: sales@loew-cornell.com
❧ *Paint brushes*
❧ *Sea sponges*
❧ *Splattering brush*
❧ *Chacopaper (water-erasable tracing paper)*

MOSAIC MERCANTILE
P.O. Box 78206
San Francisco, CA 94107
Tel: 877 966-7242
Fax: 415 282-5413
www.mosaicmercantile.com
❧ *Italian vitreous tiles*
❧ *Mosaic tools*
❧ *Mosaic glues and grout*

POLYFORM PRODUCTS CO.
1901 Estes Avenue
Elk Grove Village, IL 60007
Tel: 847 427-0020
Fax: 847 427-0426
www.sculpey.com
❧ *Polymer clay*
❧ *Polymer clay tools*
❧ *Etruscan Motifs polymer clay molds*

POLYMERIC SYSTEMS, INC.
723 Wheatland Street
Phoenixville, PA 19460
Tel: 610 935-1170
Fax: 610 935-7123
www.polymeric.com
❧ *Kneadatite (kneadable epoxy putty)*

PRESSED PETALS
47 S. Main Street
Richfield, UT 84701
Tel: 800 748-4656
Fax: 435 896-6760
www.pressedpetals.com
❧ *Pressed flowers*

SANDTASTIK
P.O. Box 1621
Niagara Falls, NY 14302
US Tel: 800 845-3845
US Fax: 716 833-3501
CN Tel: 905 734-7340
CN Fax: 905 734-7733
www.sandtastik.com
❧ *Colored sand*

SAKURA OF AMERICA
30780 San Clement Street
Hayward, CA 94544
Tel: 510 475-8880
Fax: 510 475-0973
www.gellyroll.com
❧ *Permanent markers*

UCHIDA OF AMERICA, CORP.
3535 Del Amo Boulevard
Torrance, CA 90503
Tel: 800 541-5877
Fax: 800 229-7017
www.uchida.com
❧ *Erasable fabric marker*

WALNUT HOLLOW FARM, INC.
1409 State Road 23
Dodgeville, WI 53533
Tel: 800 950-5101
Fax: 608 935-3029
www.walnuthollow.com
❧ *Wooden surfaces, plaques, boxes*
❧ *Wooden letters and embellishments*

THE WARM COMPANY
954 E. Union Street
Seattle, WA 98122
Tel: 800 234-9276
www.warmcompany.com
❧ *Fusible adhesive*

INDEX

GIVE YOUR HOME AND GARDEN A PERSONAL TOUCH WITH STYLE!

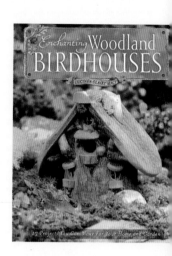

Try any of these 20 decorative mosaic projects! Each one includes step-by-step instructions, materials lists and templates you can enlarge and trace. There's no tile to cut and no messy grout. Just pick a project and get creative! From garden stepping stones to tabletops, you'll find beautiful mosaic projects for every part of your home.

ISBN 1-58180-129-7, PAPERBACK, 128 PAGES, #31830-K

Use polymer clay to create elegant décor for your home! These 19 step-by-step projects make getting started easy. You'll learn how to combine clay with fabric, silverware and other household items, plus metallic powders that simulate colored glass, antique bronze or gleaming silver. You'll also find instructions for color mixing, marbling and caning.

ISBN 1-58180-139-4, PAPERBACK, 128 PAGES, #31880-K

You can make your own tabletop fountains and add beautiful accents to your living room, bedroom, kitchen and garden. These 15 gorgeous step-by-step projects make it easy, using everything from lava rock and bamboo to shells and clay pots. You'll learn to incorporate flowers, driftwood, fire, figurines, crystals, plants and more.

ISBN 1-58180-103-3, PAPERBACK, 128 PAGES, #31791-K

Create rustic, whimsical houses perfect for use indoors and out. Lucinda Macy provides step-by-step instructions and full-color photos that make every project easy. There are 13 designs in all, including birdhouses, decorative fairy and gnome homes, and garden homes for toads. Each one can be embellished with acorns, moss, seed pods, twigs and other natural materials.

ISBN 1-58180-071-1, PAPERBACK, 128 PAGES, #31793-K